MW01120254

WILDFIRE!

A Study of Heat and Oxidation

Developed by
The Agency for Instructional Technology

JOIN US ON THE INTERNET
WWW: http://www.thomson.com
EMAIL: findit@kiosk.thomson.com
A service of I(T)P®

South-Western Educational Publishing
an International Thomson Publishing company I(T)P®

Cincinnati • Albany, NY • Belmont, CA • Bonn • Boston • Detroit • Johannesburg • London • Madrid
Melbourne • Mexico City • New York • Paris • Singapore • Tokyo • Toronto • Washington

ISBN: 0-538-66847-4

2   3   4   5   6   7   8   PR   02   01   00   99   98

Printed in the United States of America

International Thomson Publishing

South-Western Educational Publishing is a division of
International Thomson Publishing, Inc.

The ITP trademark is used under license.

This book is printed on recycled, acid-free paper that meets
Environmental Protection Agency standards.

PROJECT DESIGN

Chief Consultant
Marvin Druger, Ph.D.
Department of Science Teaching
and Department of Biology
Syracuse University

Instructional Designer
Diana W. Lee, Ph.D.
Agency for Instructional Technology

Project Developer
Jonathan Greenberg, Ph.D.
Agency for Instructional Technology

PROJECT MANAGEMENT

AGENCY FOR INSTRUCTIONAL TECHNOLOGY

Director of Projects and New Products
Frank J. Batavick

Project Management Specialist
Diane Sumner

Formative Evaluation
Rockman et al.

Administrative Assistant
Connie Williamson

SOUTH-WESTERN

Vice President/Editor-in-Chief
Peter McBride

Product Manager
Thomas A. Emrick, Ph.D.

Project Manager
Karen Roberts

Editor
Tim Bailey

Marketing Assistant
Kris M. White

SCIENCE LINKS REVIEWERS

Gary Abbas, West High School, Davenport, Iowa; **Robert Allen**, Victor Valley Community College, Victorville, California; **Carol Bedford**, Smart Intermediate School, Davenport, Iowa; **Jennifer Braught**, Shakamak High School, Jasonville, Indiana; **Matt Braught**, Linton-Stockton High School, Linton, Indiana; **Glenda Burrus**, Pinetown High School, Pinetown, North Carolina; **Laine Gurley-Dilger**, Rolling Meadows High School, Rolling Meadows, Illinois; **Ron Endris**, Floyd Central High School, Floyds Knobs, Indiana; **Sheila Engel**, Smart Intermediate School, Davenport, Iowa; **Tom Ervin**, North High School, Davenport, Iowa; **Marcy Gaston**, Pike High School, Indianapolis, Indiana; **George Hague**, St. Mark's School of Texas, Dallas, Texas; **Mary Halsall**, Hughes Center, Cincinnati, Ohio; **Craig Leonard**, Abraham Lincoln High School, San Francisco, California; **Ann Lumsden**, Florida State University, Tallahassee, Florida; **Jim Oberdorf**, Lincoln High School, San Francisco, California; **Jan Pierson**, Bloomington North High School, Bloomington, Indiana; **Eva M. Rambo**, Bloomington South High School, Bloomington, Indiana; **Willa Ramsay**, Madison High School, San Diego, California; **Kathleen Schuehler**, Liverpool High School, Liverpool, New York; **Len Sharp**, Liverpool High School, Liverpool, New York; **Dwight Sieggreen**, Cooke Middle School, Northville, Michigan; **Gerald Skoog**, Texas Tech University, Lubbock, Texas; **Ernestine B. Smith**, Tarboro High School, Tarboro, North Carolina; **Charlotte St. Romain**, Carenco High School, Lafayette, Louisiana; **Denise Tompkins**, Southwest Edgecomb High School, Pine Tops, North Carolina; **Kevin Tsui**, Woodside High School, Woodside, California; **Rick Wells**, Central High School, Davenport, Iowa; **Eric Worch**, Indiana University, Bloomington, Indiana

VIDEO AND PRINT DEVELOPMENT

VIDEO

Executive Producer
David Gudaitis, Ph.D.

Associate Producer
Brad Bloom

Scriptwriter
Bob Risher

Video Editors
Amy Crowell
John MacGibbon

PRINT

Senior Editor
John Pesta

Safety Editor
Doug Mandt

Science Writers
Sara S. Brudnoy, Ph.D.
Herbert Gottlieb
Jonathan Greenberg, Ph.D.
Douglas Hullander
Gerald Krockover, Ph.D.
Douglas K. Mandt
Michael Svec, Ph.D.

Assessment Writers
Jennifer L. Chidsey
Laura Henriques
Margaret A. Jorgensen, Ph.D.
James A. Shymansky, Ph.D.

Layout Designer/Compositor
David Strange

Cover and Page Designer
Brenda Grannan

Print and Art Coordinator
Debbie Hanna

Wildfire!

CONTENTS

Science Links ...
Where You and Your Future Connect

You can't see them, but there are thousands of doorways in front of you . . . doors to your left, doors to your right . . . big doors, little doors, revolving doors, trap-doors . . . doors stretching into the distance as far as you can see. . . . Each of these doorways is a possibility, an opportunity for a successful and prosperous life. But most of the doors are locked. You need the right keys to open them. How many doors will you be able to open?

The more you learn in school, the more keys you will have . . . the more choices . . . the more control over your own life.

Science Links is one key to your future. In the world of tomorrow—the world of computers, robotics, the World Wide Web, gene therapy, space travel— your knowledge of science can help you keep up with the latest developments in technology. More important, it can help you find a good job and pursue a great career.

Many students consider science a difficult subject, but as you will see in this course, science can be fascinating. In *Science Links* you will learn science by doing many laboratory investigations. (Investigations that are too dangerous for the classroom will be demonstrated in video segments.) These experiments will help you understand scientific principles.

YOUR LINK TO SCIENCE

Science is an attempt to make logical sense out of the natural world. It generally involves observations, experiments, data collection, analyses, and logical conclusions. *Science Links* will let you experience science, and the experience will be informative, interesting, and fun. You will be doing many laboratory investigations that will demonstrate the importance of science in your life, both now and in your future career. Following one or more investigations, a brief reading will explain the scientific principles further.

This course gives you a great opportunity to learn about science, but the learning is up to you. Learning science can be challenging, but if you work at it, you can master the contents and processes of this fascinating field. Put your full effort into this course and you will gain the satisfaction of learning many useful things about science. More important, you will advance to the next level of your education with greater confidence, a better self-image, and a strong motivation to learn even more.

So work hard, and enjoy your *Science Links* experiences.

—Professor Marvin Druger, Past President
National Science Teachers Association

Professor Druger teaches biology at Syracuse University, where he is also chairperson of the Department of Science Teaching.

Wildfire!

You will perform most of your investigations as a member of a small group. After your group completes its work, you and your teammates will have an opportunity to present your findings to the other students in your class. In the real world—the world of work—many jobs are based on teamwork, men and women working together to solve problems and share information.

In a few years you will be joining the adult workforce. *Science Links* can help prepare you for that important step in your life.

To give you a broad introduction to science, *Science Links* blends biology, chemistry, physics, and earth/space science into a single course. You will learn how various scientific concepts are used in the everyday world, both at home and in the workplace.

This book and the related video segments will also show you how science is used in dozens of careers, from food science to auto mechanics, from welding to respiratory therapy. Check out these careers. Maybe one of them is right for you.

When you picked up this book, you picked up a golden key. Use it now. Open the *Science Links* door, and step right in to the amazing world of science.

★ Log It!

As you perform the investigations in *Science Links*, you will record various kinds of information in a logbook. Use your logbook to take notes, to collect data, and to enter your observations and conclusions about the experiments you perform. The logbook is also a great place to jot down any questions and ideas that occur to you, either inside or outside the classroom. Put them on paper before you forget them!

If you get in the habit of using your logbook, it will help you learn to express your thoughts simply and clearly—that's good writing. The logbook will also give you a permanent record of your work—that's good science.

For more suggestions on using your logbook, see Appendix A (pages 76–77). The appendix also contains a sample logbook page.

Safety Symbols

TAKE appropriate precautions whenever these safety symbols appear at the beginning of the Step-by-Step instructions. All safety icons that apply to a particular investigation appear at the beginning of that investigation. In addition, a step number that is printed in red indicates the first time a certain kind of safety hazard exists in an investigation.

 ### Disposal Hazard

- Dispose of this chemical only as directed.

 ### Fire Hazard

- Tie back hair and loose clothing.
- Do not use a burner or flame near flammable materials.

 ### Eye Hazard

- Always wear safety goggles.

 ### Poison Hazard

- Do not chew gum, drink, or eat in the lab.
- Keep your hands and all chemicals away from your face.

 ### Inhalation Hazard

- Avoid inhaling the substance.

 ### Thermal-Burn Hazard

- Wear gloves and do not touch hot equipment.

 ### Breakage Hazard

- Do not use chipped or cracked glassware.
- Do not heat the bottom of a test tube.

Corrosive-Substance Hazard

- Wear safety goggles and a lab apron.
- Do not touch any chemical.

IN CASE OF EMERGENCY . . .

Immediately report any accident, injury, or spill to your teacher. Know where to find the nearest fire blanket, fire extinguisher, eyewash, sink, and shower.

Here's what to do:

Fire—Turn off all gas outlets and unplug all appliances. Use a fire blanket or fire extinguisher to smother the flames. When using a fire blanket or extinguisher to smother flames, take care not to cut off or impede the victim's air supply.

Burn—Flush the affected part with cold water.

Poisoning—Take note of the substance involved and call the teacher immediately.

Eye Injury—Flush eyes with running water; remove contact lenses. Do not allow injured persons to rub their eyes if a foreign substance is present.

Fainting—Open a window or provide fresh air as best you can. Position the person so the head is lower than the rest of the body. If breathing stops, use artificial respiration.

Spill on Skin—Flush with water.

Minor Cut—Allow to bleed briefly and then wash with soap and water. If necessary, apply a bandage.

Remember to call your teacher right away in any emergency!

module 2

WILDFIRE!

FIRESTORM

Do you live near a forest? Some parts of the country are covered with trees, but other parts have hardly any. Why is that?

Have you ever been near a forest fire? If not, you've probably seen forests burning in movies or on TV. In the video segment for Section 1 of this module, you'll see gigantic fires, with flames hundreds of feet high. The wind carries burning debris for miles, starting new fires. But some fires burn slowly and are hard to detect. Some even burn underground for months! Why is water used to put out fires? Why does water always seem to cool things off? You will learn about all of this in Section 1.

Why does a fire burn?

Exactly what is fire? How does it spread? How do firefighters try to control it? What happens after a fire—will trees grow back, or will a meadow replace the forest? You'll discover more about heat and the chemistry of fire in Sections 2 and 3.

Things get hot in this section, but they cool down too. You will explore burning, freezing, and other kinds of changes. Now, as you watch the first video segment, think about what fire actually is.

FREEZE FRAME

Now that you have seen the video segment, discuss the following on-screen questions with the other students in your class.

1 What might be some reasons that a surface fire occurs in one place and a crown fire in another?

2 Why are crown fires so intense and fast-moving?

INVESTIGATION 1

What Kind of Place Is This?

EVER WONDER?

The video segment showed forest fires in Wyoming and grassland fires in California. A grass fire is very much different from a forest fire. Have you ever wondered why forests grow in one place, grasses in another, and desert plants somewhere else? This investigation will help you understand why.

STEP-BY-STEP

Working with your group, examine the maps of rainfall, temperature, and vegetation patterns in the continental United States (see Figure 1). Compare these maps to determine why different kinds of vegetation are found in different places. (The following questions will help you do this. Group members should collaborate on answering the questions, and one member should write down the group's answer to each question as the investigation proceeds.)

1 What is the basic pattern on the map of vegetation regions? (In other words, is the map divided into forest and other zones? If so, do these regions run in certain directions, such as east-west or north-south? Describe the pattern of vegetation regions.)

2 Look at the map of average January temperatures. Is it divided into zones that run north-south or east-west? Is this pattern similar to the pattern of the vegetation regions? If not, describe the differences.

3 Now look at the map of average July temperatures. Is the pattern similar to what you found on the vegetation map? If not, describe the differences.

Continued on page 4

Science L i n k s

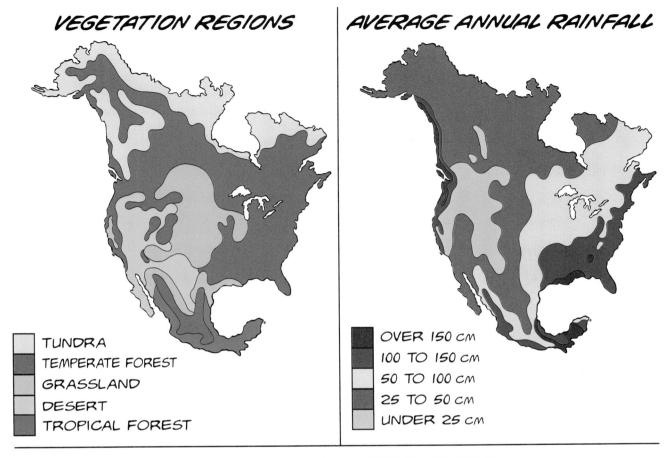

VEGETATION REGIONS

TUNDRA
TEMPERATE FOREST
GRASSLAND
DESERT
TROPICAL FOREST

AVERAGE ANNUAL RAINFALL

OVER 150 CM
100 TO 150 CM
50 TO 100 CM
25 TO 50 CM
UNDER 25 CM

AVERAGE TEMPERATURE

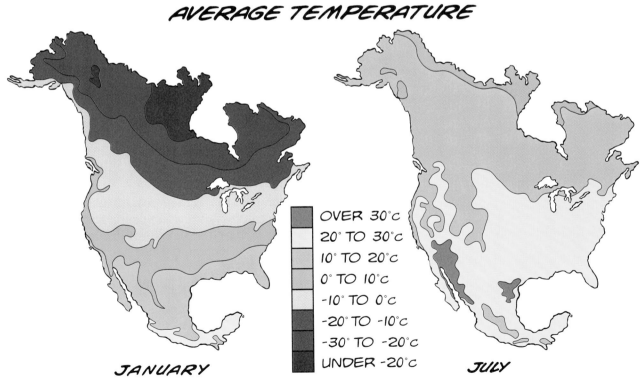

OVER 30°C
20° TO 30°C
10° TO 20°C
0° TO 10°C
-10° TO 0°C
-20° TO -10°C
-30° TO -20°C
UNDER -20°C

JANUARY

JULY

Figure 1: Maps of vegetation regions, rainfall, and temperature in the continental United States, Canada, and Mexico

4 Does temperature appear to be an important factor in controlling what kinds of vegetation will grow in a certain area? Explain your ideas, using the evidence you collected in Steps 2–3.

5 Compare the rainfall map with the vegetation map. Do you see any similarity in the patterns? Is the vegetation map more like the rainfall map or the temperature maps? Explain your ideas, using the evidence you gathered from the maps.

TALK IT OVER

Work with the other members of your group to answer the following questions.

1 Imagine you're in a brand-new Mustang . . . you have the time and money to drive all over the U.S.A. . . . Do you think you would see more change in vegetation if you drove south from North Dakota to Texas, or if you traveled west from New York to California? Give your reasons.

2 Comparing trees with grasses, which would you expect to use more water per square mile of land? Explain.

3 Do forests or grasslands provide more fuel for fires? Why?

4 Agriculture is a major industry in some states. Apples come from New York and Washington, peaches from Georgia, oranges from Florida, and many kinds of fruit from California. The midwestern states produce huge quantities of grain crops, such as corn and wheat, which are members of the grass family. What have you learned that can explain why fruit trees are grown in some places and grain crops in others?

PALM TREES IN IRELAND

Palm trees in Ireland?

Ireland is farther north than the United States, where palm trees grow only in such warm-climate states as Florida and California. Palm trees would never survive in northern states, such as New Hampshire, Pennsylvania, or Minnesota. So how can they grow in Ireland?

Although Ireland is closer to the north pole, it has a milder climate than most of America. The southwestern part of Ireland has lush subtropical vegetation. If you visit the Lakes of Killarney and the Mountains of Kerry, you will see not only palm trees but also Mediterranean trees, rhododendrons, and other plants that usually grow only in countries much farther south.

Such species can grow in Ireland because the country has a mild, wet climate all year

long, thanks to the North Atlantic Current. This current is a warm ocean stream that flows from the Gulf of Mexico north past Ireland. During the winter, westerly winds blow across the current and bring warm air to the country. During the summer, ocean waters are cooler than the land, and the winds that blow across the stream help to keep temperatures mild. The ocean winds also bring a large amount of rain to the island, and palm trees thrive in a warm, wet climate.

SPREAD THE WORD

Decide how you will present the results of your investigation to the class. To make the presentation more effective, you could display a poster with enlarged copies of the maps you used in the investigation, or you could show the maps on an overhead projector. Be sure to describe some practical applications for what you have discovered. Include information about one or more jobs that use what you have learned.

READ ALL ABOUT IT!

The Perfect Place

WHAT determines where forests, grasslands, and other kinds of biological environments exist? Investigation 1 revealed that in North America the water supply is the most important factor in the distribution of forests and grasslands. Temperature turned out to be less important. This would seem to suggest that water is the only factor that matters very much. Can that be true?

To answer the question, think about this: As you travel north from the Great Lakes, grasslands disappear completely. If you travel still farther north, forests are replaced by short tundra plants. This shows that when the climate gets cold enough, temperature also plays a major role in determining what types of plants will grow. Tropical fruits, such as oranges and bananas, will not survive in the cornfields of Illinois, no matter how

much water they receive. That's why people in northern climates consider these fruits special and often give them as Christmas presents. For the same reason, apples, which survive cold winters in the United States quite well, are a holiday treat in Mexico.

Like fruit trees, every living thing can compete with other species most successfully in its own ideal environment. What is an ideal environment? It is the right combination of climate, soil, nutrients, light, and other factors *for a particular species*. Grass can grow on forest land, and trees can grow on a prairie, but they do not compete well with the dominant vegetation that grows there. If no one interferes with the land, those species that are best adapted to the environment will dominate, whether it is forest, grassland, tundra, or desert.

ON YOUR OWN

Answer the following questions based on "The Perfect Place."

1 If you were to travel south through Mexico or if you drove from the Mediterranean Sea to central Africa, you would go from a desert region, with only a few shrubs and grass plants, to a tropical rain forest that is full of lush vegetation. What is the most important environmental factor causing these differences?

2 Plants make their food substances inside their leaves. Deciduous trees, such as oak and maple, lose their leaves in the fall. Conifers, such as pine and spruce trees, keep their needle-shaped leaves all through the winter. How can you explain the fact that cold Canadian forests contain almost nothing but conifers?

3 People live in nearly every environment on earth. Does this agree with the idea that a species tends to live in the environment best-suited to its needs? Explain.

Pick up the Pace

EVER WONDER?

If you and your friends have ever sat around a campfire, you know that when the flames begin to burn low, someone usually jumps up and starts fanning them. This can bring a dying fire back to life. Do you know why? What controls how fast a fire burns? In this investigation you will discover a major factor that affects how a flame burns.

MATERIALS LIST

- 3 widemouthed jars with tightly fitting lids
- 3 candles
- Wooden kitchen matches
- Balance
- Aluminum foil
- Masking tape or other labels for jars
- 3 beakers (150 mL)
- Graduate cylinder (100 mL)
- Metal tongs
- Spoon or spatula
- Long-stemmed funnel
- Ashtray or other safe receptacle, such as a beaker or bucket of sand, for used matches
- Hydrogen peroxide solution
- White vinegar (acetic acid, 5% solution)
- Baking soda (sodium bicarbonate)
- Small piece of raw liver (10–20 g)
- Safety goggles
- Rubber or plastic gloves

STEP-BY-STEP

Be sure to wear your goggles during this experiment, because hydrogen peroxide can burn your eyes. If you get any of the chemical on your hands, wash it off immediately. Also be careful not to get it on your clothes—it will bleach them. Because you will be working with fire, tie back long hair and roll up loose or baggy sleeves.

1 Put on your safety goggles.

2 Label each jar as either "High Oxygen," "Air," or "Low Oxygen."

3 Cut out a piece of paper so that it is about 10 cm square. (**Math tip:** Most rulers have a centimeter scale. If yours does not, you may convert inches to centimeters: 1 inch = approximately 2.5 cm.)

4 Weigh the paper. Record the weight on your group's copy of the data form. (Leave the paper on the balance.)

5 Use a spatula or spoon to put sodium bicarbonate on the paper. Continue to add sodium bicarbonate until the balance shows a weight that is 5 g more than the weight of the paper.

6 Transfer the 5 g of sodium bicarbonate from the paper to a beaker.

7 Put the beaker of sodium bicarbonate in the jar labeled "Low Oxygen." Do not spill the beaker. (You will use the sodium bicarbonate to produce carbon dioxide gas. This gas will push some of the air out of the jar.)

8 Put on your rubber or plastic gloves.

9 Measure 30 mL of hydrogen peroxide with a graduate cylinder.

10 Pour the hydrogen peroxide into a beaker. Without spilling any of the beaker's contents, place the beaker of hydrogen peroxide in the jar labeled "High Oxygen." (You will use this to provide extra oxygen to a candle flame.)

11 Rinse the graduate cylinder thoroughly with water three times. Measure 30 mL of water with the cylinder.

12 Pour the water into a beaker. Without spilling any of the beaker's contents, place the beaker of water in the jar labeled "Air."

13 Measure 30 mL of acetic acid with the graduate cylinder.

14 Crumple up aluminum foil to make a stand for each candle (see Figure 2).

15 Position each candle in its holder firmly and securely. Place a candle and holder in each jar.

16 Light a match, and hold it by the wooden end with the tongs.

17 Light all three candles—you may need to use more than one match to do this safely.

18 Now use the tongs to hold the funnel with its stem in the beaker of sodium bicarbonate.

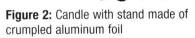

Figure 2: Candle with stand made of crumpled aluminum foil

19 Use your group's copy of the data form to write the time when the other group members begin to carry out Steps 20–22. (These three steps should be performed quickly.)

20 Pour the acetic acid through the funnel into the sodium bicarbonate.

21 Use the tongs to place a piece of liver in the hydrogen peroxide.

22 Close all three jars tightly.

23 Observe the candle flames in each jar. Write down all changes that group members observe. The time when any change occurs should also be noted. Allow the candles to burn up to 10 minutes, unless they go out sooner.

24 Blow out the candles, and rinse the beakers. Then repeat Steps 3–23 two more times. (You will need a fresh piece of liver each time.) Record your data for each jar both times.

25 Clean up your work area, and store the equipment in its proper place.

TALK IT OVER

Work with the other members of your group to answer the following questions.

1 Which candle burned for the longest time? Which burned the shortest?

2 What other differences did you observe?

3 How can you explain the differences among the three candles?

4 How can you find out if your ideas are correct?

5 Was there much change in how long each candle burned each time you did the experiment?

6 If a change occurred, how do you account for it?

7 What did you gain by performing the experiment three times?

8 The control in an experiment is the sample that the experimenter does not change in any way. It serves as a standard, and the experimental samples are compared with it. Which jar acted as the control in this experiment?

9 Why was it necessary to add water to the "Air" jar?

10 What difference, if any, would it make if you used larger candles? Explain.

11 Which candle burned fastest? Which one burned most slowly? Explain your ideas.

12 On the basis of your investigation and conclusions, what do you think controls how fast a fire burns?

OUCH!

Burns are among the most painful injuries you can get. Most burns come from hot surfaces or materials that are on fire, but direct contact with electricity and chemicals can also cause burns. If a burn is caused by hot liquids or steam, it's called a "scald."

Burns and scalds are classified according to how seriously they damage a person's skin:

- A **first-degree burn**, such as mild sunburn, damages only the surface of the skin, which becomes pink and sensitive.

- A **second-degree burn** injures the skin more deeply. Blistering, swelling, and oozing wounds may result. Examples of this type of burn are severe sunburn, bad scalds, and wounds caused by burning materials.

- A **third-degree burn** penetrates every layer of skin and even damages underlying tissue. The skin becomes white, extremely red, or black, and the victim loses the sense of feeling in the injured spot.

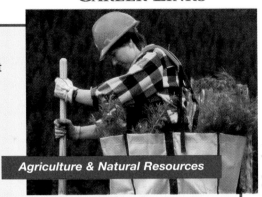

Agriculture & Natural Resources

FIREFIGHTER

Firefighters need to think about oxidation and the factors that affect the rates of oxidation reactions. When battling a fire, they must often make quick decisions that have important consequences. Firefighters may work in cities, in forests, on ships, or in other places. For more information, write:

International Association of Firefighters
1750 New York Avenue, N.W.
Washington, DC 20006

Related occupations: chemist (develops fire retardants), fire safety inspector, forest ranger

---

13 How do your results help explain how wind can speed up the burning of a forest fire? Why does fanning a fire help it to burn?

14 Car engines are designed to allow mechanics to adjust the percentages of air and gasoline in the mixture that the engine burns. Explain how the concentrations of air and gasoline affect how well the mixture burns in the engine.

RESULTS SPREAD THE WORD

Share the results of your investigation with your class. You could begin a presentation by showing your equipment and telling how you set up the investigation. Display a chart or bar graph of your results, and use it to explain what you learned about fire. Also tell how this information can help people control fires.

Think of at least one household device that uses the principles you have learned. Also describe how your findings could be used in the workplace.

READ ALL ABOUT IT!

It May Not Look like Fire, But . . .

WHEN a candle or a piece of paper or a tree burns, the object that is on fire combines with oxygen in the air, releasing energy. This is called oxidation. Some oxidations don't look anything like fire. For example, when a piece of metal reacts with oxygen in the air to form rust, it is oxidizing. *You* are oxidizing too: When the carbohydrates and fats in your body combine with the oxygen you inhale, they produce carbon dioxide (CO_2) and release energy. The oxygen that you breathe keeps this process going, and it provides all the energy you need to stay alive.

The starting materials in a chemical reaction, such as the fuel and oxygen in a fire, are known as reactants. During the reaction they change to different substances, which are called products. Fires have many products. (Can you identify some of them?) The rate of chemical reaction is the amount of a reactant that changes to products per unit of time. For instance, if a large fire burns 60 kg of wood in five minutes, you could state the rate of reaction as 12 kg per minute.

SPEED IT UP

Like other chemical changes, oxidation can be fast or slow. The rusting of iron and steel is too slow to see. The burning of a tree in a forest fire is a faster reaction. Explosions, such as those involving a bottle of nitroglycerin or the gunpowder in a rifle cartridge, are extremely fast reactions. Why do these oxidations occur at such different rates? What controls the rate of a reaction?

In Investigation 2 the concentration of a reactant (oxygen) controlled the rate of reaction in a candle flame. In general, the greater the concentration of reactants, the greater will be the rate of reaction and the amount of product formed. This is true for most reactions, not just oxidations.

Welders take advantage of this principle of concentration. They use a tool called an oxyacetylene torch (see Figure 3). This device has two tanks, one containing oxygen and one containing a flammable fuel gas known as acetylene (oxygen + acetylene = oxyacetylene). Twin nozzles release the two gases close together, creating an extremely hot flame. The flame becomes so hot because the oxygen tank provides a much greater amount of oxygen than ordinary air contains. This is another example of how

Figure 3: Welder using an oxyacetylene torch (close-up shows twin nozzles of the torch)

the concentration of reactants controls the reaction rate.

Reactant concentration affects the rate of any reaction, not just oxidation reactions. For example, if you mix vinegar and baking soda, one of the products is a gas that bubbles up through the mixture, creating a foam. The more vinegar and baking soda you use at the start, the faster these substances will produce the gas. This shows that a greater reactant concentration produces a faster reaction

CHARGE IT UP

Concentration is not the only thing that can speed up a reaction. Just as heat energy is needed to start a fire, most chemical reactions need some kind of energy boost to get going. In fact, some reactions need such a big energy boost that it is difficult for them to occur at all. That's when it helps to have a catalyst. A catalyst is a substance that reduces the energy needed to start a reaction and is not changed by the reaction. By lowering the energy needed for a reaction to begin, the catalyst speeds up the reaction and allows it to occur at a lower temperature. The reaction does not consume the catalyst—it can be used again. For example, it is easier to light charcoal than wood because charcoal (partially burned wood) contains ashes that act as a catalyst.

Catalysts are at work in your body. Living cells produce protein catalysts called enzymes, which control reaction rates. Enzymes are sensitive to concentrations of reactants and products in cells, and so they maintain fairly constant reaction rates, responding quickly to cells' needs.

ON YOUR OWN

Refer to "It May Not Look like Fire, But . . . " to answer the following questions.

1 You may have used hydrogen peroxide (H_2O_2) to clean a cut. Or maybe it's one of the ingredients in your toothpaste or mouthwash. Hydrogen peroxide is unstable: By itself, it slowly breaks down into oxygen gas and water. If you put a piece of raw liver or potato in a glass of hydrogen peroxide, the breakdown occurs faster, and you will see oxygen gas bubbling away. What are the reactants, products, and catalysts in this reaction?

> ### GET THIS . . .
> The products of fire are
> - Carbon dioxide gas
> - Water vapor
> - Carbon particles (in ashes and smoke)
> - Unburned minerals (in ashes and smoke)
> - Partly burned carbon compounds (in ashes and smoke)

2 What reactants, products, and catalysts are involved in baking a loaf of bread or a cake? (Hint: Examine the ingredients listed on the bread wrapper or on the side of a box of cake mix, or look at the ingredients in a cookbook recipe.)

3 As a forest grows, people cut down some of the trees to produce lumber and paper. Think of the forest as a gigantic set of chemical reactions. What reactants, products, and catalysts can you identify?

4 How do the amounts of reactants affect the rate at which products are produced?

5 Have you ever heard someone say, "That's like pouring fat on the fire"? What does this expression mean? Using what you have learned about chemical reactions, explain how adding fat would affect a fire.

INVESTIGATION 3

Blues in a Beaker

EVER WONDER?

Some forest fires spread so fast that it's difficult to stay ahead of them. Others smolder for days or weeks. Why do chemical changes, such as burning, occur rapidly in some cases, slowly in others? Is there anything you can do to speed up the changes you want and to slow down the ones you don't want, such as wildfires? In this investigation you will examine some of the factors that affect the rates of chemical reactions.

MATERIALS LIST

- Copper(II) sulfate (CuSO$_4$) chunks
- Copper(II) sulfate (CuSO$_4$) crystals, ground to a fine powder
- 4 beakers (each 400 mL)
- 2 hot plates
- Oven mitts or thermal gloves
- Safety goggles

STEP-BY-STEP

1 Put on your safety goggles.

2 Place an equal amount of water in two beakers (two-thirds full).

3 Set the beakers in a spot where they will not be disturbed.

4 Add 5 g of large blue crystals of the copper(II) sulfate to one beaker of water. (Simply drop in the crystals. Do not stir.)

5 Record in your logbook any changes that you observe.

6 Carefully and slowly add the fine crystals of copper(II) sulfate to the second beaker. (Let them settle to the bottom. Do not stir.)

7 Observe for several days. Record any changes. Meanwhile, continue with Step 8.

8 Repeat Steps 1–6 with two other beakers.

9 Place these beakers on hot plates with the temperature setting on medium or medium-high. Heat them steadily, but do not bring them to a boil. *Caution: By the end of the investigation, the beakers may be too hot to hold with your bare hands. Use oven mitts or thermal gloves to handle the hot beakers. If you aren't careful, you can get serious burns from the glass or the hot plates.*

10 Observe the changes that occur in the beakers as the temperature increases.

11 Disposal: When you have finished, pour all of your solids and solutions into a collection jar marked "Copper Sulfate." (Your teacher will recycle these materials so that they are not wasted or dumped.)

12 Finish cleaning your work area, and wash your hands thoroughly.

TALK IT OVER

Work with your partner to answer the following questions.

1 How did the changes in the hot beakers compare with the changes that occurred in the beakers that stayed at room temperature?

2 How could the increase in temperature have caused the changes you observed?

Science L i n k s

3 What effect did the size of the crystals have on these changes? How do you explain this?

4 Try to think of other examples of chemical changes that are affected either by temperature or by the size of the pieces of material. What are they?

5 When you watched the opening video segment, you may have noticed that some tree trunks survived the forest fire but their small twigs were gone. How can your results help explain this?

6 Which do you think would burn faster, 10 kg of dry grass or a 10-kg log? Explain.

7 Extremely hot fires, such as the 1988 Yellowstone fire in the video, cause more destructive chemical changes in trees and soil than fires that are not so hot. How can your results help explain this?

8 How can your results help explain why people need to chew their food?

MATH TIP: VOLUME AND SURFACE AREA

Try this: Start with a block of something you can cut up easily, such as cheese or milk chocolate—or arrange some small cube-shaped blocks to form a larger cube.

Measure the lengths of the sides, and use the following formula to calculate the volume and surface area of the whole block.

height (cm) x length (cm) x width (cm) = volume (cm³)

To measure the surface area of each face of the block, use this formula:

length (cm) x width (cm) = area (cm²)

Add up the areas of all six faces to find the surface area of the entire block.

Write down the volume and surface area of the block. Then divide it into 4–8 smaller blocks. Find the surface area and volume of each small block. Add up the surface areas of the small blocks. Add up the volumes of the small blocks.

When you divide a large object into small parts, what happens to its volume? What happens to its surface area?

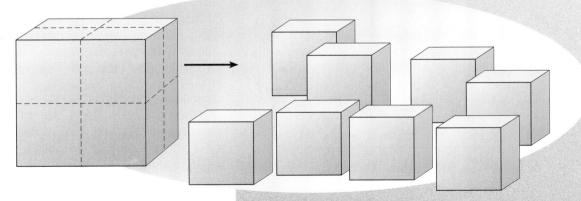

Does the total volume of the small blocks equal that of the large one? What about surface area?

SPREAD THE WORD

Give the class a presentation of the results of your work. To help other students understand, you could display the large and small pieces of copper sulfate.

Explain what you have learned about chemical change and how this knowledge may be useful. Also explain how your findings can help people understand forest fires.

Then describe how your findings are applicable in the workplace or some other practical situation.

READ ALL ABOUT IT!

What Makes Fire?

For fire to occur, three things must be present: fuel, oxygen, and heat. The fire triangle below illustrates the relationship among these three items (see Figure 4). If any one of them is missing, there can be no fire. For example, the center of a large tree contains plenty of wood to serve as fuel, but not much oxygen. Only the surface of the tree is in contact with the oxygen in the air; therefore, the center of the trunk cannot burn until the outer layers have burned away. Here's another example: Fires are less likely to start during cool weather. Why? Because the hotter the fuel is, the faster it will burn. One important lesson you should learn from the fire triangle is that the supply of fuel, oxygen, and heat controls how quickly the fuel will burn up.

GET THIS . . .

Three factors that affect the rate of a chemical reaction are
- Reactant supply
- Surface area
- Temperature

Fires burn faster at higher temperatures. In fact, the rates of most chemical reactions speed up when the reactants are heated. A hotter bonfire burns more quickly . . . an oven set at 350 degrees cooks a frozen pizza faster than an oven set at 300 . . . milk spoils faster on the table than in the refrigerator. . . . What's behind all this? The answer is that at higher temperatures the molecules of reactants move more quickly, which makes them collide more often and with greater force. As a result, there are more collisions with enough energy to break up the molecules or to recombine them to form new products.

Surface area also affects the rate of reaction. Food cooks more quickly if it is cut up. Each cut exposes more surface area to the heat. As you watched the video about forest fires, you may have noticed that the small branches and twigs burned quickly and the big branches and trunks burned more slowly (see Figure 5). To understand why, suppose you tried to

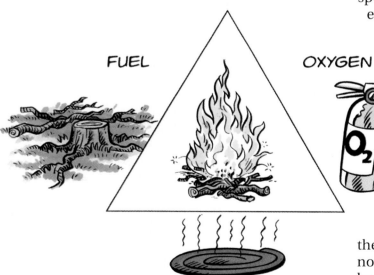

FUEL   OXYGEN

HEAT

Figure 4: The fire triangle

burn a 1-kg bundle of twigs and a 1-kg block of wood. The twigs would have much more surface area in contact with the air, and this would make them burn faster. In other words, the surface area of a solid reactant helps to determine its rate of reaction. A heavy iron fence or a ship's anchor may take years to oxidize (rust), but a wet scouring pad of fine steel wool can rust in a day or two. Similarly, your body can digest food more quickly and completely if you chew it into small pieces, because smaller pieces have more surface area exposed to the fluids in your digestive system.

Figure 5: Trees whose small branches burned because they had more surface area per gram than the trunks

ON YOUR OWN

Answer the following questions based on "What Makes Fire?"

1 Using your knowledge of chemical reactions, explain how refrigerators and freezers keep food from spoiling.

2 When burning wood, people usually start with paper or twigs and let these materials light the bigger logs. Why does it help to start with smaller materials?

3 Farmers sometimes find that they must provide their animals with more feed in the winter if they expect the animals to grow as fast as they do the rest of the year. How does your knowledge of chemical reactions help explain this?

4 Some cake icings are made by mixing a large quantity of sugar with a small portion of milk or butter to make a smooth paste. Why would a baker use powdered sugar instead of granulated sugar to make icing?

CAREER LINKS

FOOD SCIENTIST

A career in food science usually requires a four-year college degree. Many food scientists also have graduate degrees. They may work in manufacturing or do research. For more information, including a booklet on food technology, write:

Institute of Food Technologists
221 N. LaSalle Street
Chicago, IL 60601
http://www.ift.org

Related occupations: food-product designer, meat and poultry inspector, restaurant inspector

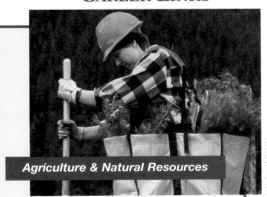

Agriculture & Natural Resources

Reaction in a Bottle

EVER WONDER?

If you ever watched the flames at a cookout or barbecue, you probably noticed that the fire reduced the wood or charcoal to a small pile of lightweight ashes. Similarly, huge trees weighing several tons seem to vanish in a forest fire—all that's left is a thin layer of ash. Where did all that wood go? Can a chemical change, such as burning, make material (matter) disappear? In this investigation you will look for evidence that can help you decide if matter can be created or destroyed during a chemical change.

MATERIALS LIST

- Baking soda (sodium bicarbonate)
- Graduate cylinder (25 mL)
- Spoon or spatula
- White vinegar (acetic acid, 5% solution)
- Beaker (250 mL)
- 2 large test tubes (25 mL or larger)
- Plastic soda bottle with screw cap (2 L)
- Balance
- Safety goggles

STEP-BY-STEP

As two group members begin this investigation at Step 1, the third member should begin at Step 13.

1 Put on your safety goggles.

2 Cut out a piece of paper that is approximately 5 cm square.

3 Weigh the paper. Record the weight on your group's copy of the data form. (Leave the paper on the balance.)

4 Use a spatula or spoon to put baking soda (sodium bicarbonate) on the paper. (Continue to add sodium bicarbonate until the balance shows a weight that is 2 g more than the weight of the paper.)

5 Transfer the 2 g of sodium bicarbonate from the paper to the bottom of a 250-mL beaker.

6   Measure 20 mL of vinegar in a graduate cylinder.

7   Pour the vinegar into a test tube.

8   Set the test tube in the beaker. (Be careful not to let any vinegar drip on the baking soda.)

9   Weigh the beaker with all of its contents. Record the weight.

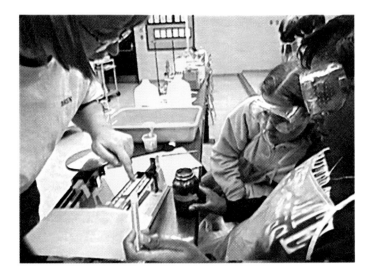

10 Pour the vinegar into the beaker. Observe the reaction.

11 When the production of gas has stopped, place the test tube in the beaker again.

12 Weigh the beaker and its contents after the reaction stops. Record the weight.

13 Cut out a piece of paper that is approximately 5 cm square.

14 Weigh the paper. Record the weight. (Leave the paper on the balance.)

15 Use a spatula or spoon to put 2 g of sodium bicarbonate on the paper. (Continue adding sodium bicarbonate until the balance shows a weight that is 2 g more than the weight of the paper.)

16 You now have 2 g of sodium bicarbonate. Transfer this material from the paper to the soda bottle.

17 Measure 20 mL of vinegar in a graduate cylinder.

18 Pour the vinegar into a test tube.

19 Slide the test tube into the bottle. (Be careful not to spill any of the vinegar.)

20 Place the cap on the bottle, tightening it firmly.

21 Weigh the bottle and its contents, without spilling any of the vinegar. Record the weight.

22 Now tip the bottle so that all the vinegar pours out and mixes with the soda.

23 Weigh the bottle and its contents. Record the weight.

24 Carefully open the cap and release the gas. Rinse and dry the bottle and the test tube.

25 Clean up your work area, and store all the equipment in its proper place.

Wildfire!

TALK IT OVER

Work with the other members of your group to answer the following questions.

1 How much did the weight of the open beaker and its contents change during the reaction? How much did the weight of the closed bottle change during the reaction?

2 How do you account for any difference in how the two weights changed? (This question refers only to the change in weight, not the total weight of the two containers.)

3 What do you think happened to the weight that "disappeared"? Do any of your observations support your idea?

4 What do your results tell you about whether material is created or destroyed during a chemical change?

5 When an intense fire reduces a forest to ashes, what happens to the material that makes up the trees? Do the ashes weigh as much as the trees did? If not, where did all that material go?

6 When a forest grows back after a fire, trees that will eventually weigh hundreds of pounds begin to grow again. Where does all the new material in these trees come from?

7 As you grow, your weight increases. Where does the new weight come from?

8 People often lose some weight while doing strenuous exercise or while working in hot places. Does the weight just disappear? What happens to it?

GOING UP IN FLAMES

Since the late 1950s, approximately four million acres of land have burned in wildfires in the United States each year. Does that sound like a lot? Back in the 1930s more than 10 times that much forest land burned in some years. Wildfires became less common until the huge forest fires of the late 1980s and '90s. And to put this in perspective, the Great Black Dragon Fire of 1987 in Siberia and northern China burned 18 million acres, making it the biggest forest fire ever recorded.

—Adapted from Temperate Forest Foundation, *Eco-Link* 4 (no. 4): 6.

SPREAD THE WORD

Decide how you want to present the results of your investigation to the other students in your class. You might begin by describing how the reaction looked and how you used the open and closed containers.

Explain what you have learned about chemical change.

Show the class how much the weights changed. Then tell how your findings on chemical change may be useful at home or in different jobs.

Where'd All the Trees Go?

AFTER an intense fire, even a thick forest may seem to have vanished, leaving only a thin layer of ashes. Were all those large trees reduced to feathery dust? How can that be? The Law of Conservation of Matter states that matter cannot be created or destroyed. Yet the ashes obviously weigh a lot less than the trees did! Where did the rest of the material go?

Well, even though it looks as if most of the material in the trees simply disappeared, actually all of it still exists—somewhere. Part of the material was converted to ashes, carbon dioxide gas, and water vapor; part of it blew away in the form of smoke and settled back to earth, possibly miles away; and some may have been washed away by rain. But nothing just disappeared!

ON YOUR OWN

Answer the following questions based on "Where'd All the Trees Go?"

1 How can an acorn grow into a huge oak tree without violating the Law of Conservation of Matter?

2 Is it possible to harvest vegetables on a field every year without ever adding fertilizer?

3 Some kinds of plants accumulate large quantities of toxic metals that have been dissolved in the water in the ground. Could these plants be grown in contaminated soil as a way of cleaning that soil? What problems do you see in this approach to cleaning up land that is polluted by chemicals?

IT'S THE LAW—OR IS IT?

According to the Law of Conservation of Matter, the amount of material contained in a substance involved in a chemical reaction will be exactly equal to the amount of material in the products of that reaction. For example, if you burn a chunk of coal, you will produce three products: carbon dioxide gas, water vapor, and ashes. If you start out with 10 kg of coal and air, you will end up with 10 kg of carbon dioxide gas, water vapor, and ashes. The coal changes drastically, but none of its original matter is destroyed, and no new matter is created.

Scientists used to think there were no exceptions to this law—but then Albert Einstein appeared on the scene. He showed that it is possible to convert some matter to energy. This is not the same as burning a lump of coal to make heat. Einstein was talking about nuclear reactions, not chemical reactions. In a nuclear reaction, a small amount of matter is destroyed, releasing a tremendous amount of energy. (This is a special situation that occurs only in nuclear explosions and the centers of stars. It does not affect the common types of chemical reactions that you experience every day.) Scientists now follow the Law of Conservation of Matter and Energy, which means that the total amount of matter and energy in a substance before a reaction is the same as the total amount of matter and energy after the reaction.

The Egg Boiler

EVER WONDER?

Anyone who's ever tried to start a fire with wet wood knows how difficult it can be. Forest managers know that fires are less likely to start during wet weather. Why is it so hard for damp wood to get hot enough to burn? This investigation will help you answer that question.

MATERIALS LIST

- 4 raw eggs
- Beaker (500 mL)
- Cooking pot (3 L)
- 2 Celsius thermometers
- 2 hot plates
- Stirring rod
- Oven mitts or thermal gloves
- Safety goggles

STEP-BY-STEP

1 Put on your safety goggles.

2 Place 350 mL of water in the beaker and 2 L of water in the pot.

3 Using a hot plate, heat the contents of each container to the boiling point. Record the time you turn on the heat.

4 Use your logbook to record the boiling temperature of each container. Note which one takes longer to boil.

5 Turn off the hot plates.

6 Gently place two eggs in each of the containers.

7 For the next 15 minutes, slowly stir the water of each container. Make sure the eggs are fully submerged and not broken.

8 At the end of the 15-minute period, record the temperature of the water in each container.

9 Wearing oven mitts, gently pour the water into the sink and remove the eggs from the containers.

10 Crack each egg open over a sink or wastebasket. Observe.

11 Record a description of each pair of eggs, including any differences between the eggs from the beaker and the eggs from the pot.

12 Clean up your work area, and then be sure to wash your hands with soap and water. *Caution: Do not eat the eggs unless your teacher tells you they are clean and safe.*

TALK IT OVER

Work with your partner to answer the following questions.

1 Did the water in both containers boil at the same temperature? What was the temperature of the water in each container after 15 minutes of stirring?

2 Where did the heat of the water go as the water cooled?

3 Is there any difference in how well the eggs were cooked? If so, which eggs were more completely cooked?

4 Did one container of water release more heat to the eggs than the other?

5 Which container boiled first? Do you think one container of water absorbed more heat from the hot plate than the other container did?

6 Can one object absorb more heat than another yet still have the same change in temperature?

7 How does this explain why it is harder to get wet wood hot enough to burn than it is to get dry wood hot enough?

8 What is the difference between heat and temperature?

Today both men and women are on the front line fighting fires. Their jobs require them to wear and carry heavy gear.

SPREAD THE WORD

To help other students understand what you've learned in this investigation, prepare a brief presentation of your results. A poster with drawings that show how you set up the investigation and how the eggs looked at the end would be useful.

Be prepared to describe how your results can help explain the importance of moisture in forest fires.

Explain how your findings can be used in the workplace or some other real-world situation. Name different types of workers who need to understand these matters to do their jobs.

READ ALL ABOUT IT!

Be Specific

PICTURE yourself on a beautiful beach. It's a hot day, and you want to go swimming, but instead of just jumping in, first you test the water with your foot. Why do you need to do this? Shouldn't the water have the same temperature as the sand on the beach? After all, the water and sand are exposed to the same weather, aren't they?

There's a difference between land and water temperatures. It takes more energy to change the temperature of water than the temperature of sand, soil, or concrete. You must add more heat to water to heat it up. Water also releases more heat as it cools down.

The amount of heat that must be added to one gram of a substance to raise its temperature 1°C is called its **specific heat**. The specific heat of water is high, compared with that of other substances (see Figure 6). For example, water absorbs or releases more heat than soil does when the temperature changes. To put it another way, the sun may add the same amount of heat to the water and the land, but the land will get hotter. At night the land will also cool down sooner. This is why a city on the edge of the ocean usually has less-extreme hot and cold weather than a city located far inland.

A good example of a place with extreme temperature changes from day to night is a desert. The dry desert soil warms up quickly during the day, heating the air above it; but at night it cools down

fast. Deserts are often extremely cold at night.

The concept of specific heat can help you understand forest fires. Anyone who has tried to start a wood fire knows that wet wood does not burn well. The specific heat of water is much greater than the specific heat of wood, and so it takes much more

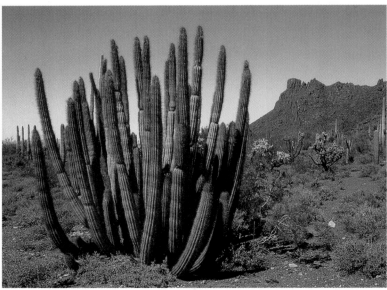

Oceanside areas (top) tend to have less variable climates than inland regions. By contrast, a desert (bottom) is very hot during the day, very cold at night.

heat energy to get damp wood hot enough to catch fire. That's why forest managers and firefighters pay close attention to the weather. If the forest gets too dry, the risk of fire jumps.

The concept of specific heat can also explain some things that occur in the kitchen. For instance, did you ever test spaghetti to see if it was fully cooked? If you did, you probably used a fork to snag a piece of spaghetti, and then you may have held the spaghetti in your bare hand and put it in your mouth, without burning yourself! But you never could have put your hand in the pot of boiling water without being scalded. The reason is that spaghetti has a lower specific heat than water. Even though the spaghetti and the water are at the same temperature, less heat energy is transferred to your hand when you touch the spaghetti than when you touch the water.

A HANDFUL OF HOT SPAGHETTI

Now think about this: Why is it that you can hold a little bit of hot food, such as one piece of spaghetti taken straight out of boiling water, without burning your hand, but you can't use your bare hands to hold all the spaghetti at once? If both items are the same temperature, what is the difference between holding one piece of food and a whole potful? The difference is that the spaghetti in the pot contains a lot more material. It can transfer more heat to your hand than one piece can. This difference is called heat capacity. The **heat capacity** of an object indicates how much heat is needed to change its temperature by 1°C. It takes more heat energy to change the temperature of a heavy object than a small one. Heat capacity is equal to the specific heat of the object multiplied by its weight. A potful of spaghetti contains far more material than a single piece, and so the heat capacity of the whole potful is greater than the heat capacity of one piece, and it can transfer that much more heat to your hands.

The concept of heat capacity also explains why a cook would boil food in a large pot of water rather than a small one with just enough water to cover the food. A big pot of water will not get any hotter than a small one, but the larger amount of water can transfer more heat to the food. Hard-boiled eggs can finish cooking after the heat is turned off—they continue absorbing heat from the hot water until they are fully cooked. Because heat capacity depends on the weight of the material, you must be sure that the pot contains enough water to provide the necessary heat.

GET THIS . . .

Heat capacity is the amount of heat that an object absorbs or releases when its temperature changes by 1°C.

Heat Capacity = Specific Heat x Weight

SOME SPECIFIC HEATS

	Material	Specific Heat (calories/gram/°C)
Earth Materials	water	1.00
	rock, sand, dry soil	0.20
Building Materials	wood (typical)	0.60
	steel	0.11
	aluminum	0.22
	brick	0.20
	concrete	0.23
	glass	0.10–0.20

Figure 6: A table of specific heats

ON YOUR OWN

Answer the following questions based on "Be Specific."

1 Many animals huddle together in cold weather. How can the concept of heat capacity help explain this behavior?

2 The cooling system of a car's engine contains antifreeze, a liquid that circulates through the engine to keep it from getting too hot. If water is used as the coolant fluid, it might freeze in the winter or boil over and evaporate in the summer. To prevent these problems, people mix antifreeze with water. Why use any water at all? Why not use pure antifreeze?

3 Many bakeries use their ovens all day long. In fact, some ovens run 24 hours a day. The oven in your kitchen is probably lined with steel. Why do so many bakeries use ovens lined with brick instead of steel?

4 You've probably had some weather when the days were much warmer than the nights. Would you expect the difference between day and night temperatures to be greater in an ocean or in the air? Explain.

SECTION WRAP-UP

Matter Matters

FORESTS can replace grasslands wherever the climate provides enough water. The water not only helps trees grow, but it also keeps their wood and leaves moist, which keeps them from burning easily. Water has a greater specific heat than wood; therefore, it takes more heat energy to heat moist wood to the burning point. This is also why the temperatures of lakes and oceans tend to change less than the temperatures of land areas.

Fire is one example of a chemical change called oxidation. This type of chemical change is oxidation because it involves material that combines with oxygen. The rate at which a fire consumes a forest (or any other fuel) depends on several factors. These include the temperature and the surface area of the fuel, as

The Law of Conservation of Matter holds true in every chemical reaction.

well as the concentration of oxygen. Fuels such as dry leaves, grass, and twigs have more surface area than tree trunks and branches of the same total weight; as a result, they burn more quickly. Fire cannot exist unless it has sufficient fuel, oxygen, and heat energy. Two other kinds of oxidation are the rusting of metal and the breaking down of food substances in your body. These oxidations also speed up at higher temperatures, higher concentrations of liquid or gaseous reactants, and larger surface areas of solid reactants.

Not only oxidations, but nearly all chemical reactions will occur faster at higher temperatures or with a greater supply of reactants. Another way to increase a reaction rate is to use a catalyst. Remember, a catalyst is a substance that speeds up a chemical reaction by reducing the quantity of energy needed to start it. Catalysts are different from reactants. Reactants are consumed or used up during the reaction, but catalysts are not; they are not even changed by the reaction. In the human body and other living things, special protein catalysts called enzymes speed up the thousands of chemical reactions that take place.

During oxidation or any other chemical change, the reactants are converted to products. For example, a fire converts a tree and oxygen from the air to carbon dioxide, water, and ashes. The products may look, feel, or smell different from the reactants. Even so, the total weight of the products is always equal to the total weight of the reactants. This principle is called the Law of Conservation of Matter. Sometimes it's not easy to find all the products and reactants: Most of the products of a forest fire are either gases or small particles of ash that the wind carries away. But the Law of Conservation of Matter holds true in every chemical reaction.

ON YOUR OWN

Answer the following questions based on "Matter Matters."

1 A sugar cube is difficult to light with a match, unless it has been rubbed with ashes. What reactants, catalysts, and products are involved in the burning of an ash-covered sugar cube?

2 Why can a fire move through grass faster than it can move through a forest?

3 Which of the following situations involve oxidation?

   a. tarnishing of silver in the air

   b. a hot glowing wire in a toaster

   c. a person doing aerobic exercises

   d. sugar dissolving in a cup of coffee

4 People at the beach during the day often run across the hot sand to get to the cooler water. Is the sand usually warmer than the water at night too? Explain.

5 How is it possible for a forest to grow back after a fire without violating the Law of Conservation of Matter?

CAREER LINKS

Mechanics & Transportation

AUTO MECHANIC

Most mechanics have one or two years of specialized training, and they must continue learning as technology changes. Auto repair requires knowledge of mechanics, electricity, physics, and chemistry. For more information, write:

Automotive Service Association
P.O. Box 929
Bedford, TX 76021

Related occupations: autoworker, automotive designer, mechanical engineer, car safety inspector

ON THE FIRE LINE

I N Section 1 you learned some important facts about where forests grow. You also learned about oxidation and other kinds of chemical change. This helped you understand what fire is and how trees burn.

For a wildfire to spread, heat must be transferred from burning vegetation to other plants that are not yet burning. In Section 2 you will discover more about how heat energy travels. This will help you understand how a fire spreads. Once you grasp this, you will be better able to stop a fire in an emergency. You will also see why the transfer of heat is one of the most important forces that shape the climate and weather.

Get ready to watch another video segment about forest fires. Observe how the fire behaves. How does it spread? Where does it grow quickly and easily? What stops it? After this segment you will get a chance to discuss these questions. Then your teacher will divide the class into groups so that you can begin your investigations of heat and temperature. Once groups share their findings, you will have a much better understanding of forest fires.

FREEZE FRAME

During this video segment, the following question appears on the screen. Work with the rest of your class to answer it.

1 Why do you think dead trees help spread fires better than living trees?

Later in the segment another question appears. Share your thoughts.

2 Why use detergent?

At the end of the segment, the screen challenges you with two more discussion questions:

3 How does water put out a fire?

4 What else does a fire need besides air?

CAREER LINKS

Engineering Technologies

IBM

HEATING, VENTILATION, AND AIR-CONDITIONING (HVAC) TECHNICIAN

HVAC technicians install and repair systems for transferring heat in or out of buildings or rooms. They must understand all three forms of heat transfer, and they must know how heat is gained or lost as coolant fluids go through phase changes. Many HVAC technicians prepare for their careers by completing one or two years of technical training after high school. Some are responsible for maintaining the environment in a specific building. Others work as independent contractors, installing or repairing heating and air-conditioning systems. For more information, write:

Air Conditioning Contractors of America
1513 16th Street, N.W.
Washington, DC 20036
http://www.acca.org

Related occupations: architect, building contractor, housing inspector, car air-conditioning technician

INVESTIGATION 6

Greasy Handles

EVER WONDER?

How do things get hot? Touching a hot stove will heat up your hand in a hurry, but exactly how does the heat move from the stove into your hand? Does it work the same way with all materials, or do some things heat up and cool down more quickly than others? In this activity you will look for answers to these questions.

MATERIALS LIST

- 2 cups or beakers (300 mL)
- Margarine (approximately 1 teaspoon)
- 1 plastic spoon
- 1 metal spoon
- Hot water (provided by teacher)
- Paper towels
- Safety goggles

 ## STEP-BY-STEP

1 Put on your safety goggles.

2 Place half of your margarine on the handle of the plastic spoon. Place the other half on the handle of the metal spoon.

3 Fill both cups with hot water.

4 Discuss these questions: If you place the scoop end of each spoon in hot water (without getting the margarine in the water), will the margarine melt? If so, will the margarine on both spoons start melting at the same time? Record your answer on the bottom of your team's copy of the data form. Also list the reasons behind your answer.

5 Place one spoon in one cup of hot water, and place the other spoon in the second cup. (Make sure the margarine itself is not touching the water.) Either you or your partner should record your observations on the data form.

6 Feel the ends of the two spoons. Record your observations.

7 Use the paper towel to clean the spoons. Follow your teacher's instructions for cleaning up your work area.

TALK IT OVER

Work with your partner to answer the following questions.

1 What happened to the margarine on the handles?

2 Describe how the heat energy was transferred from the hot water to the margarine.

3 Which spoon was more efficient at transferring heat?

4 Would it be better to eat hot soup with a metal spoon or a plastic one? Explain why you think so.

SPREAD THE WORD

Share the results of your investigation with your classmates. Start by showing how you set up and conducted the experiment.

Explain why the movement of heat through materials is important, and give some examples of how your findings are used in various jobs.

INVESTIGATION 7

Top-down or Bottom-up?

EVER WONDER?

How does fire spread through a forest? Does most of the heat travel sideways, as each burning tree sets its neighbors on fire? Does most of the heat move upward, from dead wood and dry plants on the ground into the treetops? Or does it move downward, with the top branches catching fire and then spreading the flames to dead logs on the ground?

This investigation will let you observe how heat travels, but you'll study some situations that are safer than forest fires. For example, if you put a pot of water on the stove, you can observe how the water at the top heats up. You can see how long it takes for all the water in the pot to get hot. You can also see if it makes any difference whether the water is heated from the top or from the bottom. If you ever went swimming in a lake, you probably noticed that deeper water was colder than water near the surface. Why is that so? This investigation will help you find the answer.

FIRE ZONE

Grassland fires are common in southern California. Whipped by strong Santa Ana winds, these blazes often cover thousands of acres, closing major highways and destroying homes, sometimes entire neighborhoods. In October 1993 more than two dozen wildfires consumed 173,000 acres in six counties. Firefighters battled the flames around the clock. The hot, dry winds made it impossible for them to stop the fires during the day, but they made better progress at night, when the weather was cooler and the winds lost some of their fury.

MATERIALS LIST

- Ringstand
- Celsius thermometer with temperature range over 100°
- Clamp
- Graduate cylinder (250 mL)
- Beaker (250 mL)
- Immersion heating coil
- Safety goggles
- Oven mitts or thermal gloves

Wildfire!

1 Measure 200 mL of water in the graduate cylinder. Pour the water into the beaker.

2 Insert an immersion heating coil just below the surface of the water (see Figure 7). *Caution: Do not insert the heater plug into the electrical outlet at this time. An immersion heating coil will be damaged beyond repair within a few seconds unless it is covered by water while in operation.*

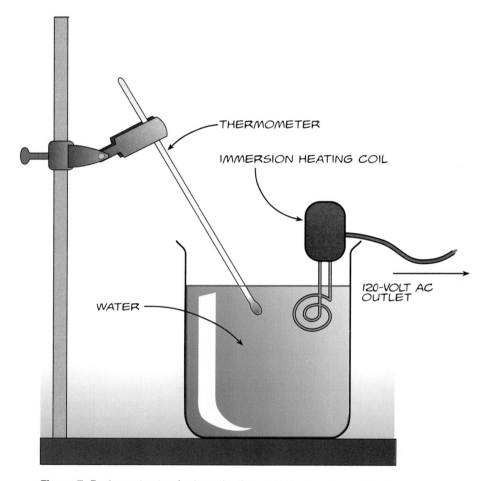

Figure 7: Equipment setup for investigating water temperature at the top

3 Working with your group, predict how long it will take for the water to start boiling. Record this prediction and the reasons for it on your group's copy of the data form.

4 Put on your safety goggles. Use a clamp and ringstand to hold a thermometer in the water, with its bulb just below the surface of the water (see Figure 7). *Caution: Make sure the thermometer does not touch the heating coil!*

5 Insert the plug of your heater into a 120-volt outlet to start heating the water. Record the time when you start heating the water.

6 Record the temperature of the water every 30 seconds until it starts to boil. (Be sure to note the temperature of the water when it starts to boil. Also note how long it took for the water to boil.)

7 Unplug the heater before you remove it from the water. *Caution: Let the heater cool down while it is still in the water.*

8 After the heater has cooled, remove it from the water.

9 Use oven mitts to pour the hot water into the sink.

10 Again measure 200 mL of cold water in the graduate cylinder. Pour the water into the beaker.

11 Replace the heating coil just below the surface of the water. *Caution: Do not insert the heater plug into the electrical outlet at this time.*

12 Insert the thermometer with its bulb at the bottom of the beaker (see Figure 8).

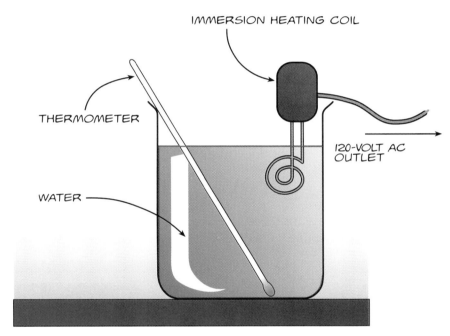

Figure 8: Equipment setup for investigating water temperature at the bottom

13 Work with your group to predict how many seconds it will take for the water to reach the boiling point in this position. Record this prediction on the data form. Also record your reasons for making the prediction.

14 Record the temperature of the water.

15 Work with your group to predict what you think the thermometer readings will be every 30 seconds from the time the heater is started until the water begins to boil. Record your predictions and reasons on your data form.

16 Insert the plug of your heater into a 120-volt electrical outlet to start heating the water.

17 Record the temperature every 30 seconds until the water begins to boil.

Wildfire!

18 Move the thermometer bulb so that it is just below the surface of the water. Observe the temperature, and record it on your data form.

19 Unplug the heater before you remove it from the water. *Caution: Let the heater cool down while it is still in the water.*

20 After the heater has cooled, remove it from the water.

21 Use oven mitts to pour the hot water into the sink. Follow your teacher's cleanup instructions.

TALK IT OVER

Work with your partner or group members to answer the following questions.

1 Compare your data with your original predictions. If any of the predictions were substantially different from the actual data, discuss the reasons for the differences with the others in your group.

2 In which part of the container did the hotter water tend to stay? What about the colder water? What are the reasons for this?

3 Can all of your observations be explained by the possibility that heat is an invisible substance that can be added to a container of water to make the water hot? Would adding something make the water heavier or lighter? Explain why adding something (heat) to cold water makes the part of the water that is heating up light enough to float to the top.

4 What conclusions can be drawn from this investigation?

5 According to your observations, where would you expect to find the coldest area of water in a pitcher of ice water?

CAREER LINKS

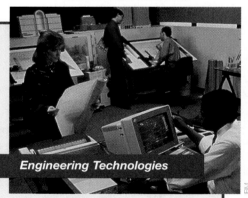

Engineering Technologies

ELECTRIC POWER ENGINEER

Electric power engineers design and maintain sources of power for communities or large factories. They must determine how much heat the systems will generate, and they have to find ways to transfer some of that heat away from the equipment to prevent overheating. Cooling systems may rely on radiant heat loss, large surface areas for convective cooling, or fans that conduct heat away by blowing air through the system. Electric power generators often use river or ocean water for cooling. For information, write:

Edison Electric Institute
Information Resource Center
701 Pennsylvania Avenue, N.W.
Washington, DC 20004-2396

Related occupations: electrician, portable-generator technician, electric heating engineer

SPREAD THE WORD

Tell the class what you discovered and how your understanding of heat transfer can help explain what you observed.

Be sure to discuss any unusual observations that surprised you during this investigation. Also show the equipment you used to conduct the experiment and explain its purpose.

Tell the class how your conclusions may be useful to a person who works with heating and cooling processes. If possible, interview a man or woman who has a job installing this kind of equipment, and report to the class what you learn.

INVESTIGATION 8

Soda in the Sun

EVER WONDER?

Suppose there's a big bonfire blazing on the beach, and even though you're standing several feet away, you feel yourself starting to sweat. . . . Or maybe you're just standing outside the mall on a nice sunny day, but after a few minutes you realize you're starting to feel warm. . . . In both of these situations, you aren't touching anything that's hot, but heat gets to you anyway. How does it reach you?

Heat travels the same way in a forest fire. Burning trees can make other trees so hot that they burst into flame. And an electric broiler in an oven can heat things up without any contact between the food and the hot, glowing wire. How does the heat from the this electrical element get to the food? This investigation will help you come up with the answers to these questions.

MATERIALS LIST

- Celsius thermometers
- 2 empty soda cans painted black or covered with black paper
- Space heater
- Meter stick
- Graduate cylinder (250 mL)
- Safety goggles

Wildfire!

STEP-BY-STEP

1. Put on your safety goggles.

2. Use the graduate cylinder to fill both soda cans with equal volumes of water.

3. Place a thermometer in each can.

4. Position one of the cans 60 cm away from and directly in front of the space heater. Position the other can 60 cm away from and directly to the side of the space heater.

5. Use your group's copy of the data form to record the temperature of the water in each can. Also record the time of these readings.

6. Turn on the space heater.

7. Leave the cans in place for as long as possible (at least 20 minutes).

8. Record the final temperature of the water in each can. Also record the time of the readings.

9. Turn off the space heater, and store all materials in their proper places.

A NEATER THEORY OF HEAT

In the seventeenth and eighteenth centuries, most scientists believed that heat was a mysterious fluid that traveled between objects of different temperatures. They called the fluid "caloric," and they thought that the temperature of an object depended on how much caloric it possessed. This explanation was good enough to explain most of the experiments that scientists performed in those days.

A cannon maker named Benjamin Thompson shot down this theory and helped develop the modern concept of heat. While operating a cannon factory in Bavaria, which is part of Germany, Thompson noticed that as long as he bored (drilled out) the metal gun barrels, they kept getting hot, until all the metal wore away. He realized that if caloric were a real substance, all of it should eventually be released and the metal should stop getting hot, even if the drilling continued. But this never happened.

The caloric theory was dead.

Thompson led an unusual life. He was born in Massachusetts in 1753, when the American colonies were ruled by Great Britain. After serving as a spy for the British governor of New Hampshire, he moved to England when the Revolutionary War broke out. There he served as a government administrator and began conducting experiments with gunpowder.

He joined the British army and rose to the rank of colonel. Later he sought to make his fortune on the mainland of Europe. In Bavaria his efforts to eliminate begging and improve the lives of poor people led the ruler of that country to make him a count (a position of nobility). Thompson chose the name "Count Rumford" because his wife had been born in the town of Rumford, New Hampshire.

Both as a soldier of fortune and as a scientist, Benjamin Thompson knew how to make a name for himself.

TALK IT OVER

If you performed this experiment with a partner, work together to answer the following questions.

1 How long were the cans heated? What was the change in temperature for the water in each can? Was the water in both cans warmed equally? If not, which one was warmed more? How do you explain this?

2 How was the heat transferred from the space heater to the water in the can?

3 Could you build a similar device that would heat water for your bathtub? Draw or describe how such a device would work.

SPREAD THE WORD

Present the results of your work to the other students in your class. Demonstrate how you set up your equipment, or provide a drawing of how you arranged it.

Tell what you discovered about how heat travels. Also tell how your understanding of this concept can help explain what you observed. Be sure to discuss any observations that surprised you during the investigation.

Describe how your conclusions could be useful to a person with a job that involves heating and cooling.

READ ALL ABOUT IT!

Turning Up the Heat

HAVE you ever gone ice skating or sledding in the middle of winter, on a day when the temperature plunged far below freezing? Your skin became red and raw; your perspiration froze; and the wind clawed at your face.

Do you know why you felt so cold that day? It's because your body is warmer than the air around it. When two objects are touching each other, the warmer one heats the cooler one until they reach the same temperature. Your body is doing its best to warm up the air, but unfortunately there's way too much air for your body to heat up. As heat flows out of your body, your temperature drops.

What happens when one object heats another? At one time scientists thought heat was an invisible substance that traveled between objects that had different temperatures. Benjamin Thompson disproved this theory (see "A Neater Theory of Heat," page 34). Today scientists define heat as a form of energy, not a substance. Heat comes from the moving atoms and molecules that make up everything. These particles move at different speeds in different kinds of matter. The faster they move, the higher their temperature. **Temperature** is a measurement of the average energy of these particles.

When energy in the particles travels from one place to another, it is called **heat**. When a hot, burning branch touches an unburned limb, the molecules at their surfaces are in contact. The molecules of the hot branch are moving faster than those in the unburned wood. They have more energy. Every time they collide with molecules in the cooler branch, some of their energy is transferred to those molecules. It's like what happens when a fast-moving bumper car hits a slower one and makes it go faster. Because hot and cold molecules are colliding millions of times per second, the average speed of the molecules in the cooler wood increases—the branch heats up. At the same time the hot branch, which is giving up energy, cools down slightly. The cooler branch may become hot enough to burn. Heat transfer by contact is called **conduction**.

RISING AND RADIATING

A second type of heat transfer is convection. To understand how convection works, look at what happens when something, such as a pot of water, is heated from below (see Figure 9). As a liquid gets hotter, its molecules move faster and spread out. The fluid expands, becoming less dense. If you mix hot and cold water, the cooler, denser water tends to sink and the warmer water tends to float to the surface. (Have you ever heard the expression "Heat rises"?) When water is heated from below, the water on the bottom gets hot first and rises to the surface. When it's on the surface, it cools off somewhat, as a new layer of water on the bottom heats up. Eventually the cool surface water sinks, and the new hot water rises from the bottom. This produces a cycle. The tendency of hot fluids (liquids and gases) to rise is known as **convection**.

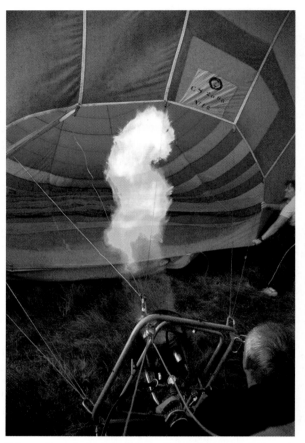

When the air inside this balloon is heated, the air molecules move apart, making the hot air less dense than the surrounding air. The hot air rises; the surrounding air sinks beneath it; and the balloon goes up. A balloon will never get off the ground if it weighs more than the air it displaces.

The third type of heat transfer involves heat in motion through open air or empty space. Think about the heat you feel from the sun on a bright day—or how a toaster works. The sun does not actually touch you, and the bright orange wires in the toaster do not actually touch the bread. So how does heat energy travel from one to the other? You may have noticed that objects that emit heat usually produce light too. This is not a coincidence. These objects produce rays of light energy that spread out or "radiate" in all directions. They also produce rays of heat that radiate in the same way. No solid, liquid, or gas is needed to carry the heat energy. It can travel through matter or through a vacuum, just as heat from the sun

Figure 9: Convection cycles

travels through outer space. Heat rays warm any object that absorbs them. This type of heat transfer is known as **radiation**.

Like light, heat radiation is pure energy—it has no substance, no weight. (By the way, heat radiation is not the same as nuclear radiation, which can be extremely dangerous.) Because everything has some temperature and at least some heat energy, all objects radiate heat energy. The warmer an object is, the more heat energy it radiates.

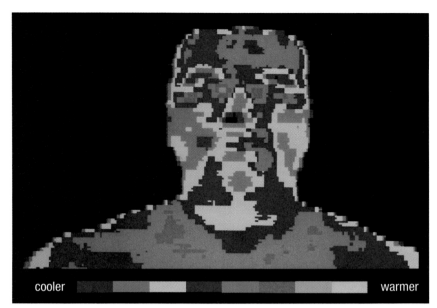

cooler   warmer

Because the human body emits radiant heat, doctors and other health professionals can use this heat to make thermographic images. In a thermogram each color represents a different temperature. In this thermogram of a patient's face, each color signifies a difference of 1°C. The cooler colors near the mouth and above one eye may indicate that these parts of the face are not receiving enough blood flow.

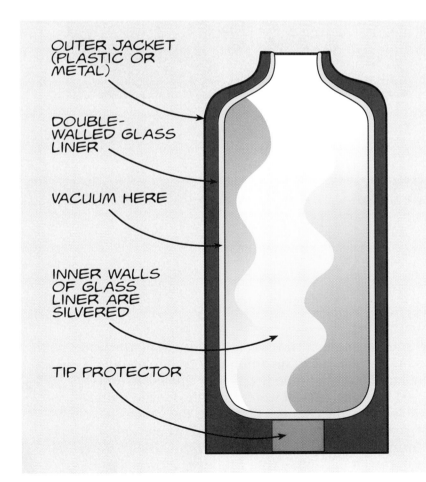

OUTER JACKET
(PLASTIC OR
METAL)

DOUBLE-
WALLED GLASS
LINER

VACUUM HERE

INNER WALLS
OF GLASS
LINER ARE
SILVERED

TIP PROTECTOR

BOTTLED UP

How does a thermos bottle keep milk cold and coffee hot? A thermos bottle is actually a bottle within a bottle, separated by a vacuum. The thermos maintains the temperature of its contents by reducing all three kinds of heat transfer. Its silver-coated inner surface reflects radiated heat back inward, and the vacuum between the inner and outer bottles reduces heat loss caused by convection and conduction.

ON YOUR OWN

Answer the following questions based on "Turning Up the Heat."

1 Give three examples of heat transfer by convection.

2 Which form or forms of heat transfer make people feel warm in a crowded room? Explain your answer.

3 How is heat energy transferred to a person's body by a heat lamp?

4 What happens at the atomic level when two objects of different temperatures are touching each other?

INVESTIGATION 9

Hot Ice

EVER WONDER?

Before damp wood and moist green leaves can burn, must all the water they contain evaporate? It takes a certain amount of heat to change things from solid to liquid or from liquid to gas. This applies to everything, whether it's fuel for forest fires or water from the faucet. In this investigation you will explore the changes that occur in water as heat is added, and you will see what happens to temperature when water changes from one form to another. Afterward, when you discuss the results with your group, you should apply your findings to forest fires.

MATERIALS LIST

- Hot plate
- Celsius thermometer
- Beakers (150 mL)
- Small bowl
- Stirring rod
- Ice and water (or crushed ice)
- Graphing paper
- Graduate cylinder (100 mL)
- Safety goggles

STEP-BY-STEP

1 Use the graduate cylinder to measure 100 mL of ice and water (or crushed ice).

2 Transfer the ice to the beaker.

3 Measure the initial temperature, and record the reading on your group's copy of the data form.

4 Put on your safety goggles.

5 Place the beaker on the hot plate, and put the thermometer in it.

6 Turn on the hot plate to a high setting.

7 Have one group member measure the temperature of the water. Record the reading on the data form.

8 Continue to measure the temperature of the water every 30 seconds and to record these readings on the data form. Take readings until most of the water is gone. Stop before the water level falls below the top of the thermometer bulb. Mix the water continuously with the stirring rod. Do not use the thermometer as a stirring rod. *Caution: Be careful while stirring the water—the steam rising from the beaker will be hot enough to burn you.*

9 Turn off the hot plate before the water level gets down to the thermometer bulb. Let the beaker cool down. Do *not* pour out the water until the beaker has had time to cool.

10 After the beaker cools, pour the water into the sink and rinse the beaker. Put away your materials.

11 Make a graph of your results. (**Math tip:** Show the time on the horizontal or x-axis and the temperature on the vertical or y-axis. Designing graphs is an important math skill. If you need help, ask your teacher to show you how to make various kinds of graphs, or see the feature "How to Make a Line Graph" on page 4 of *Science Links* Module 1.)

TALK IT OVER

Work with your partner(s) to answer the following questions.

1. Did the temperature change much during the first few minutes on the hot plate? Is this what you expected? Explain.

2. Could you have a mixture of ice and water that is colder than 0°C? Explain your answer.

3. Did you expect the temperature of the water to rise above 100°C? Explain your answer.

4. Did the temperature ever rise above 100°C? Explain why.

5. Look at your graph. It shows temperature and elapsed time. On this kind of graph, how can you identify the boiling temperature and freezing temperature of a liquid?

6. During the time when the temperature did not change, was the hot plate still transferring heat to the water? If it was not raising the temperature, what was happening to the heat energy?

7. Water boils at 100°C, but wood must be much hotter than that to start burning. How can this investigation help you explain why wet wood is hard to burn?

BURNING IDEAS

Ray Bradbury wrote a novel called *Fahrenheit 451*. It depicts a society in which people do not have the freedom to read whatever they want. In an effort to control everyone's beliefs, the government confiscates all banned books and burns them.

There's real science behind the title of this science-fiction novel. The title refers to the fact that many kinds of paper catch fire when they reach a temperature of 451°F (232°C). The temperature at which a substance bursts into flame is called its "kindling point." Every burnable material has its own kindling point.

CAREER LINKS

OIL REFINERY WORKER

Petroleum is a complex mixture. Refineries separate it into different products, such as gasoline, kerosene, and motor oil, by heating it to carefully controlled temperatures. These temperatures are chosen so that some compounds in the mixture will be liquids and others will evaporate. The gas is collected and cooled so that the desired compounds condense as liquids. Workers must understand these phase changes. Some workers have a high school diploma; others have a college degree. For more information, write:

American Petroleum Institute
1220 L Street, N.W.
Washington, DC 20005
http://www.api.org

Related occupations: ethanol-plant worker, automotive engineer, desalination-plant operator, water distiller

Agriculture & Natural Resources

U.S. Forest Service

SPREAD THE WORD

Give a presentation of the results of your investigation. You could start by showing the class your equipment and displaying your graph. Be sure to explain what the graph represents.

Describe how your conclusions may be useful in various jobs involving temperature. These jobs may involve boiling, melting, or freezing, all of which are caused by changes in temperature.

FROSTY FRUIT

When the air temperature falls below the freezing point of water (0°C), plants are in big trouble. At subfreezing temperatures, the fluids inside their cells freeze and expand, rupturing the cell walls. They are victims of a "killing frost."

Farmers can lose money if frost strikes their crops. To help protect their strawberries, orange trees, and other crops, farmers sometimes spray them with water. The water soon freezes, encasing the plants in ice! What's going on here? If the farmers are so worried about cold temperatures, why do they cover their crops with ice?

Many people think the ice serves as an insulator, protecting the plants from air that is even colder than the ice. But it's not that simple. Here's what's really going on:

Even after water gets cold enough to freeze, it must give up a great deal of heat energy to change from a liquid to a solid (ice). The water transfers this heat energy to whatever it is touching. As the water freezes on the trees, heat energy passes from the water to the trees, keeping them a little warmer.

The sprayed water also falls onto the ground, where it freezes, donating heat energy to the soil. In turn, some of the heat in the soil then rises into the branches. This process also helps keep the branches from freezing.

Spraying water protects plants only from temperatures that are a few degrees below freezing, and only for a short time. If the spraying continues too long, it may damage plants, because the weight of the ice can break the branches.

Wildfire!

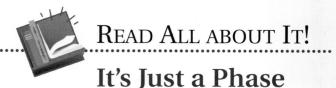

READ ALL ABOUT IT!

It's Just a Phase

SOLIDS, liquids, and gases are the three phases of matter. **Phase change** occurs when something freezes, melts, or boils. It might surprise you to learn that when a phase change occurs, the temperature of the substance that is changing stays about the same. Sound confusing? After all, if you want to change water from a liquid to a gas, don't you heat it until it boils? Where does the heat energy go when the water finally reaches the boiling point and the change occurs?

To understand why the temperature barely changes when a phase change occurs, remember that the particles (atoms or molecules) that make up matter are attracted to one another. When a solid **melts** or a liquid **evaporates**, its particles gain energy. This energy allows the particles to overcome the forces of attraction, just as a rocket engine provides the energy needed to overcome the force of gravity and lift a spaceship off the ground. When you melt ice, you are adding heat energy, but that energy does not raise the temperature (see Figure 10).

Instead, it gives the water molecules enough energy to break free from one another. As each molecule breaks loose, it leaves the solid ice and begins to move around as part of the liquid. Finally, the last bit of ice melts. At that point, all of the molecules have overcome the forces that held them together in the form of ice.

Keep in mind that when you add heat energy, you increase the speed of the molecules, which is measured as temperature. Once all the ice has melted, any additional heat energy that you add to the now-liquid water *will* increase its temperature.

THE OTHER WAY

What about phase changes that go the other way, from liquid to solid or from gas to liquid? A change from gas to liquid is called **condensation**. Have you ever noticed that a cold bottle of soda gets wet—some people say it "sweats"—while it stands on a table? Moisture appears on the bottle because its surface is cold enough to make water vapor from the air condense into a liquid. The

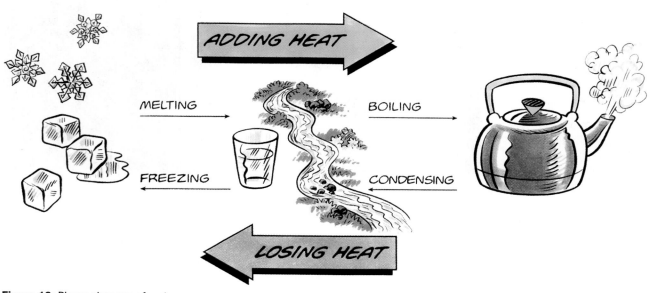

Figure 10: Phase changes of water

Science L i n k s

same thing happens when you take a hot shower—the bathroom mirror fogs up. Here's why: Part of the warm shower water evaporates into the air. When some of this water vapor touches a cooler surface, such as the bathroom mirror or walls, it condenses as tiny liquid droplets. The warm molecules of water in the air have more energy than the molecules in the cold surface. The soda bottle or bathroom mirror gains a little energy from the water and becomes slightly warmer. The water molecules lose a little energy—enough for some to slow down and change from a gas to a liquid.

The same thing occurs when liquids change to solids. This process is called freezing. On a cold night after it rains, a street surface may get cold enough to freeze water. In the puddles on the street, water molecules collide with pavement molecules. Because the pavement is colder than the water, the pavement molecules have less energy. Every time a water molecule and a pavement molecule collide, some energy passes from the faster-moving water molecule to the slower-moving pavement molecule. Eventually some of the water molecules lose so much energy that they slow down enough to stick together, forming solid ice—and dangerous driving conditions. When temperatures fall below freezing after a rainstorm, you've got big problems.

Ice forms in various ways. The ice crystals in the snow on the branches (left) formed directly from water vapor in clouds. The icicles above the stream (right) formed from liquid water dripping off rocks.

ON YOUR OWN

Answer the following questions based on "It's Just a Phase."

1 Can you tell the temperature of ice water without measuring it? Explain your answer.

2 When you make ice in a freezer, what happens to the heat energy that the water loses when it freezes?

3 When a patient has an extremely high fever, a doctor or nurse may give that person an alcohol rubdown. Does alcohol on the skin actually make a person cooler? Explain how evaporating alcohol takes heat energy from the body.

4 If you work in a fast-food restaurant, you know that some foods are cooked in deep fryers. Why is frying faster than boiling?

Wildfire!

What Makes the Weather?

EVER WONDER?

Heat transfer, in all three of its forms, occurs all around you all the time. As you read this sentence, your body is warming your chair by conduction; it's warming the air by convection; and it's warming your classmates by radiation. In a sense, you are changing the weather around you. The weather outside also changes because of heat transfer. In this investigation, which is based on a video demonstration, you will see what makes the weather.

READ ALL ABOUT IT!

Weather Report

As you saw in the video demonstration, temperature, humidity, wind, and rain can all be explained by heat transfer, specific heat, and phase changes. The sun is the earth's main source of energy. The sun makes the earth warm enough to support life, and it provides the driving force that changes the weather. The sun radiates heat, which warms the ground on earth. Solar radiation then leads to heat transfer by conduction and convection: Air near the ground is heated by conduction and rises, carrying heat energy up through the atmosphere by convection. As the warm air rises, other air follows to take its place: High, cool air descends toward the ground. This process creates wind. Wind is moving air. (If you've ever spent time on the eastern

side of a tall mountain range, you probably experienced cold winds blowing downhill, even on a warm day.)

Does it matter whether the wind blows across land or water before it reaches you? Some water is always evaporating from lakes and oceans. Air that travels over water absorbs some of that water vapor. This has two important effects on the weather near the water.

First, moist air is more likely to produce rain, fog, or snow than dry air that has passed over land. This is why such cities as San Francisco, Chicago, and Buffalo have damp climates—they are located next to large bodies of water.

Second, because water has a greater specific heat than soil or rock, oceans and lakes tend to change temperature more slowly than dry land does; therefore, oceanside and lakeside areas do not experience the same extremes of high and low temperature as dry areas. This is one reason Los Angeles is cooler than the desert to the east and Boston has milder winters than the western, inland parts of Massachusetts.

Answer the following questions based on "Weather Report."

1. Bombay, India, is on the shore of the Indian Ocean. New Delhi, the capital of India, is about 580 miles from the ocean. Which city would you expect to receive more rain? Explain why you think so.

2. London, England, is about 20 miles from the North Sea. The difference between the average London temperature in January and July is 13°C. Kiev, the capital of Ukraine, is about 275 miles from the Black Sea. Would you expect there to be a larger difference between average summer and winter temperatures in London or in Kiev?

3. What are two ways that the sun contributes to the formation of rain clouds?

4. In coastal areas it is common for breezes to blow in from the water toward the land during the day. But at night the breezes blow out from the land toward the water. How would you explain this?

SECTION WRAP-UP

Heating Up, Cooling Down

EVERYTHING is made of atoms and molecules that are constantly moving and colliding. Temperature is a measurement of the average energy of all those moving particles in one place or in one object. When this energy is transferred from one place to another, it is called heat.

Heat energy can be transferred in three ways: conduction, convection, and radiation. In a forest fire, wood and leaves heat up by touching other material that is already burning. This transfer of heat energy by contact is called conduction. When conduction occurs, energy is transferred from a warm object to a cooler one that it is touching. Each time the molecules at their touching surfaces collide, the faster-moving, "hotter" molecules slow down a bit, and some of their energy is transferred to the slower-moving, "cooler" ones, which speed up. Eventually the two objects can reach an intermediate temperature, if nothing else is adding or removing energy from them.

> **Everything is made of atoms and molecules that are constantly moving and colliding.**

A second form of heat transfer is convection. If you understand convection, you know why smoke and flames travel upward in a forest fire. As the air around the fire heats up, its molecules gain energy. They speed up and spread out from one another over a larger volume. This increase in volume reduces the air's density, and it begins to float up over the cooler air above. The cooler air sinks down to where the fire is. It then begins to heat up there, while the warmer air above begins to cool. A cycle develops in which air becomes warmer in the fire near the ground, rises, cools, and then falls again. The rising hot air and smoke heat the branches above the fire until they begin to burn. This helps to spread the fire to the tops of the trees. It also creates winds that carry away bits of burning branches, which start new fires. Crown fires are intense, and they move fast.

An intense fire creates enough heat to ignite neighboring trees, even if they are several meters away from the flames. This occurs because the molecules of burning wood radiate heat energy. The other trees absorb enough of this energy to reach the temperature at which they begin to burn. Radiation releases heat in the form of rays that can travel through air or a vacuum until they reach an object, which absorbs the energy. This raises the temperature of that object. Everything radiates some heat energy, but burning wood releases enough to spread the fire—or to warm people sitting around a fireplace.

THREE PHASES OF MATTER

Solids, liquids, and gases are called the three phases of matter. Living trees contain some liquid water. In a forest fire, as the flames heat living trees, this water begins to evaporate. The temperature of the wood will not rise above 100°C until the water completely evaporates. But the wood can't burn until it gets much hotter than that. The water helps to protect the trees from fire. Here's how: The molecules of a substance are attracted to one another. In a solid the attraction holds all of them close together. In a liquid the molecules have enough energy to separate and move around somewhat. In a gas they have enough energy to escape their attraction almost completely. Whenever water (or anything else) changes from one phase to another, it gains or loses heat energy. By raising or lowering the temperature of a substance, you can cause it to change from one phase to another.

Whenever water (or anything else) changes from one phase to another, it gains or loses heat energy.

Once the fire has heated a tree to 100°C (the boiling point of water), any additional heat energy that the tree absorbs will increase the energy of water molecules. Each water molecule in the liquid phase gradually gains enough energy to escape from its attraction to the others and break free as water vapor. Once all of the water molecules have evaporated, the wood can absorb any additional heat from the fire. Eventually it too may become hot enough to burn.

These phase changes are reversed when a substance cools. As wind and convection carry water vapor away from the fire, the water molecules lose energy by radiation and conduction. If they slow down (cool) enough to cling together loosely, they condense as drops of rain. If the water molecules slow down still more, they hold one another together closely and the water becomes solid—it freezes. These changes happen to other things besides water. When any pure substance gains or loses enough energy, it will change phase at specific temperatures, namely the melting point and the boiling point of the substance. Water (ice) melts at 0°C and boils at 100°C. Other substances have their own melting and boiling points.

On Your Own

Answer the following questions based on "Heating Up, Cooling Down."

1 During the winter you may have noticed that the roofs of some houses had more snow on them than others did, even though they had the same slope. What does this mean? Would it be better to live in a house with more snow on the roof or in one with less?

2 Radiators and machines that produce a lot of heat often have many thin plates or fins on their surfaces. How do these plates help transfer heat energy to the air?

3 People occasionally need to store something at a constant temperature. A container of water can be used to do this, provided the temperature is moderate. Why would it be a bad idea to use water to maintain the temperature of a hot or cold object? What solutions to this problem would you suggest?

4 Many animals that live on land have evolved ways to control their temperatures. Plants do this too. They absorb water through their roots, and it travels upward through trunks and stems to the leaves. Water evaporates through tiny openings in the leaves. Does this keep the plants warm or cool? How does the evaporation of water cause the leaves to gain or lose heat energy?

Section 3

Part 1:
WASTELAND

IF you were to walk through a forest after a fire, you might wonder how anything could ever grow there again. Yet somehow plants begin poking through the blanket of ashes, and soon animals start wandering into the area to feed on the plants.

This raises many questions: Will the great trees of an old forest ever grow back, or will the new trees be smaller and take longer to grow? What are ashes made of, and how do they affect the growth of the new plants? In such a barren-looking place, how will the new plants find all the nutrients they need? Without a canopy of leaves to protect it, will the soil (and its plant nutrients) be washed away before anything can grow? And what's so important about the soil anyway?

You will investigate these questions in Section 3, which has two parts. Start by watching the next video segment, which shows how a forest looks after a fire and how it begins to recover. As you watch, look for patterns in the way the vegetation grows back. Also see if you can come up with a few ideas that help explain how these changes occur.

 FREEZE FRAME

Discuss the following on-screen questions with the other members of your class.

1 How could the land be damaged by a forest fire?

2 What is the sequence of plant regrowth after a forest fire?

Acids or Ashes?

EVER WONDER?

After a fire, the forest becomes a different kind of place. The fire has produced a layer of ashes that seem to cover everything. What is in these ashes? How will they affect the soil? How will they affect the new plants, which begin the process of recovery? In this investigation you will compare ashes with other familiar substances, and you will discover how the kinds of materials in ashes affect living things.

MATERIALS LIST

- Dropper pipet (medicine dropper)
- 2 graduate cylinders (10 mL)
- Graduate cylinder (25 mL)
- pH paper
- Red litmus paper
- Blue litmus paper
- Stirring rod
- 10 test tubes (10 mL or larger)
- Test-tube rack
- 2 beakers (150 mL)
- Marking pencil or labels
- Forceps
- 3 flasks (125 mL) with loose covers (aluminum foil or cotton plugs)
- White vinegar (acetic acid, 5% solution)
- Lemon juice
- Apple juice
- Soap or detergent solution
- Soda pop
- Ammonia
- Liquid antacid
- Soil sample
- Ash remains from the burning of wood or paper
- Pond or stream water
- Baking soda (sodium bicarbonate)
- Spoon or spatula
- Small living pond organisms
- Microscope
- Microscope slides and cover slips
- Safety goggles

STEP-BY-STEP

While one or two group members perform Steps 1–16, the remaining member(s) should begin with Step 17. (As you carry out this investigation, be sure to rinse out the graduate cylinders after each use.)

1 Put on your safety goggles.

2 Label nine of the test tubes from "1" through "9." After labeling, place them in the test-tube rack.

3 Place soil in a beaker until it is approximately one-third full.

4 Fill the beaker the rest of the way with tap water.

5 Use a stirring rod to break up the soil and to mix it with the water. Set the beaker aside, allowing time for most of the soil to settle to the bottom.

6 Put each of the following substances into the test tube with the corresponding number. Fill the tubes approximately halfway. *Caution: Avoid inhaling ammonia fumes—they may injure your eyes and lungs.*

Tube	Test Substance
1	Lemon juice
2	Soda pop
3	Pond or stream water
4	Vinegar
5	Soap solution
6	Ammonia
7	Antacid
8	Water from soil mixture
9	Tap water

7 Tear off small pieces of red and blue litmus paper and pH paper.

8 Use the forceps, if necessary, to dip one fresh piece of each kind of paper into each sample. The pieces of paper may change color. (Compare the color of the pH paper with the color chart in the package, and note the pH number.) Enter all results on your group's copy of Data Form A.

9 Use a spatula or small spoon to add a small quantity of baking soda (about the size of your thumbnail) to each tube. Observe the results. Record observations on Data Form A.

10 Put ashes into a small beaker, filling it to a depth of 2 or 3 cm.

11 Add twice that volume of pond water to the beaker.

12 Use a clean stirring rod to mix the water and ashes.

13 Test the ash-water mixture with red and blue litmus paper, pH paper, and baking soda, as in Steps 8–9. Record the results on Data Form A.

14 Use the two smaller graduate cylinders to measure 5 mL each of lemon juice and ammonia, and combine them in a test tube.

15 Test the mixture as in Steps 8–9. Record the results on Data Form A.

16 Remember to rinse out the graduate cylinders with water.

17 Use a dropper pipet to place 1 drop of water containing pond organisms on a microscope slide.

18 Add a cover slip, and observe under the microscope at low power.

19 Make a drawing of what you observe, and record the magnification that you are using.

20 Count or estimate how many organisms you can see at one time, without moving the slide. Use your logbook to record the number of each type of organism.

21 Move the slide slightly, and repeat the tasks you performed in Step 20.

22 Move the slide again, and repeat the same tasks.

23 Record the average of all three counts.

24 Make three labels ("1 mL"; "10 mL"; "20 mL"). Attach each one to a flask.

25 Using a 10-mL graduate cylinder to measure, add 1, 10, or 20 mL of vinegar to each flask, as labeled.

26 Using a 25-mL graduate cylinder to measure, add enough pond water to each flask to bring the total volume in each flask to 45 mL. (Explanation: Add 44 mL of pond water to the "1 mL" flask; add 35 mL to the "10 mL" flask; add 25 mL to the "20 mL" flask.) Use a 10-mL graduate cylinder to add 5 mL of water containing pond organisms to each flask.

27 Cover the flasks with aluminum foil or loose cotton plugs. Set them aside in a warm sunny place where they will not be disturbed. Wash your hands with soap and warm water before leaving the lab.

28 Wait at least three days. Then place a drop from each flask on a microscope slide. Add a cover slip, and perform Steps 18–23 again. (Be sure to use the same magnification when you use the microscope.) If possible, repeat your observations three more days. After every observation enter the results on Data Form B. Be sure to wash your hands with soap and warm water every day before leaving the lab.

TALK IT OVER

Work with the other members of your group to answer the following questions.

1. Examine the information on Data Form A. Can the substances be classified into groups that share certain properties. For example, do substances with a high pH tend to react the same way to litmus paper? To baking soda? . . .

2. Are ammonia and lemon juice in the same group? What happened when you combined them?

3. How did you classify soil and pond water? How did ashes affect the pond water?

4. Examine the information on Data Form B. How did vinegar affect the pond organisms?

5. Substances with pH below 7 are called acids. Substances with pH above 7 are called bases. Pure water, with a pH of 7, is neutral—it is neither an acid nor a base. (You'll learn more about acids and bases later.) Are ashes acidic or basic?

6. Does the survival of living things depend on their pH? Is it likely that all living things require the same pH range?

7. What would be the effect if rain washed ashes into a pond after a forest fire?

8. What effect would ashes have on soil and plants after a forest fire?

9. From what you have learned in this investigation, would you expect the plants that grow back after a fire to be the same kind that grew in the forest before the fire?

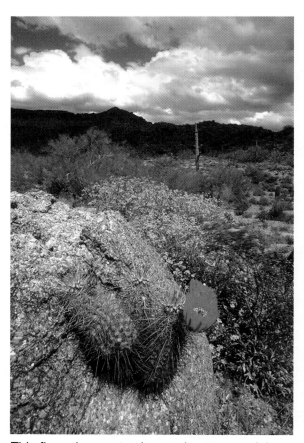

This flowering cactus is growing on a rock in the desert. Many desert soils are so basic that few plants can grow there. Most of the bases in soil are mineral compounds that dissolve in water. Because deserts receive little water, bases build up in the soil. Only plants that have adapted to these harsh conditions can survive.

SPREAD THE WORD

RESULTS

Much of your testing involved color and color change. Make a color chart, table, or other diagram to make it easier for the class to understand the results of your investigation.

Present your ideas about how important acids and bases are to living things, particularly in the workplace. You might also present a game show at the end of your talk: Have your classmates guess which substances are acids or bases, and then let them verify their guesses with indicator paper.

Tell how what you have learned can be applied at home or in various jobs.

Science L i n k s

READ ALL ABOUT IT!

What's an Acid?

You probably know that a water molecule is made of two hydrogen atoms and one oxygen atom: H_2O. Wherever water is present, a few of these molecules break apart to form hydrogen ions (H^+) and hydroxyl ions (OH^-). Many substances, including most soils, produce additional hydrogen ions. These substances are called acids. Substances that produce hydroxyl ions are called bases.

Acids and bases are opposites: When an acid and a base are mixed together, the two types of ions combine to form water, and the acid and base cancel each other out—they "neutralize" each other.

The pH scale is a convenient way to describe acids and bases: Pure water, which is considered neutral, has a pH number of 7. Acids are numbered below 7 (the more acidic the solution, the lower the pH number). Bases are numbered above 7 (the more basic the solution, the higher the pH number).

Acid rain causes serious damage to forests and lakes, especially in the northeastern United States.

All living things have an ideal pH range in which they grow best. Many of the nutrient minerals that trees and other plants extract from the soil are bases. As the forest grows, a great deal of the supply of basic minerals moves from the soil to the trees and other plants. This process leaves the soil increasingly acidic.

After a fire, much of the basic mineral supply remains in the ashes. When rain washes the ash minerals back into the ground, the soil pH rises. Now the plants that begin the recovery process can start to grow. These plants, which include grasses, are known as pioneer species because they are the first to occupy the land.

The growth of many species is affected by pH. Have you ever heard of "acid rain"? This condition causes serious damage to forests and lakes, especially in the northeastern United States. The U.S. Fish and Wildlife Service has developed a chart to show how different levels of acidity kill various kinds of animals that live in ponds and streams (see Figure 11).

HOW pH AFFECTS ORGANISMS

pH	Unable to Survive
6.0	Clams and snails die. (Most fish survive.)
5.5	Crayfish, mayflies, rainbow trout, and small-mouth bass die.
5.0	Brown trout, sunfish, and spotted salamanders die.
4.5	Brook trout, yellow perch, bullfrogs, and toads die.
4.0	All fish and wood frogs die.
3.0	Nearly all aquatic animal life dies.

Figure 11: Effect of pH level on life of organisims

Wildfire!

ON YOUR OWN

Answer the following questions based on "What's an Acid?"

1 Which of the following might be acids: HF, HCl, FeS, CuO, or H_2CO_2? Explain your reasons for selecting them.

2 What would you expect to be the pH of a mixture of equal quantities of acid and base?

3 Some lakes in the Adirondack Mountains of northern New York state have been so damaged by acid rain that they are sterile—nothing can live in them. Suppose you could add something to the water to help repair the damage. Which of the following is most likely to help make the pH level close to neutral: NaCl, NaOH, HCl, or Na_2SO_4? Explain your choice.

4 Sometimes acids, such as vinegar, or bases, such as ammonia, are used as cleaners. Could you make a stronger cleaner by combining vinegar and ammonia? Explain your answer.

CAREER LINKS

RESPIRATORY THERAPIST

A respiratory therapist needs to understand the chemistry of acids and bases. Why? A patient with a respiratory (breathing) problem may also develop a blood problem, because poor breathing increases the acidity of blood. A respiratory therapist provides treatment under the supervision of a doctor: Medical tests are given; breathing is measured and analyzed; and therapies are administered. Because therapists work closely with patients and doctors, they must also have good communication skills. To become a therapist, you must have either a two-year associate's degree or a four-year bachelor's degree. With a two-year degree, you would engage in direct patient care; the four-year degree would equip you to become a department manager. For more information, write:

American Association for Respiratory Care
11030 Ables Lane
Dallas, TX 75229

Related occupations: air-quality inspector, pulmonary specialist (lung doctor), paramedic

Health & Human Services

Part 2: OUT OF THE ASHES

G ET ready to see the final video segment of this module. It will show you how a forest grows back after a fire. As you watch, think about the effects of a forest fire. Is every forest fire a disaster, or is it a good thing for a forest to burn?

AIT Video

FREEZE FRAME

Now that you have seen how a forest comes back to life after a fire, discuss the following on-screen questions with the rest of the class.

1 Why are some forest fires set on purpose?

2 Should forest fires be allowed to burn? Explain.

I N V E S T I G A T I O N   1 2

Changes in a Microworld

EVER WONDER?

Do you know who the first people were who lived where you live today? Over the centuries, one group followed another, right up to your own family and yourself. American Indians . . . pioneer settlers . . . farmers and ranchers . . . city dwellers and suburbanites . . . one group gave way to the next. Each group changed the place—the environment—in some ways, and these changes made the place attractive to a new group. Living things constantly change their environments. This allows some species to increase, while others become rare or disappear.

In the video, you saw how a forest starts to grow back after a fire. First, grasses and other small plants rise through the ashes. This vegetation is

Wildfire!

replaced by bushes and small trees. Later, taller trees with leafy branches replace the smaller ones. . . . Whether grass, trees, or some other kinds of plants cover the ground, you can be sure there are animals feeding on them—and larger animals are probably feeding on the smaller ones eating the plants.

EVERYTHING IS LINKED

"When you try to change any single thing, you find it hitched to everything else in the universe."

—John Muir, American (Scottish-born) naturalist

What is the source of energy for all these plants and animals? Can changes in the environment convert a forest to a grassland or a desert? How does a stable forest change and become overrun with deer? Why doesn't this happen to every forest? You will explore these issues in this investigation—but you'll use a smaller system that changes much more quickly than a forest.

MATERIALS LIST

- 2 large beakers (250–600 mL) with covers (petri dish, watch glass, or plastic wrap)
- Small beaker (150 mL)
- Hot plate (or tripod, screen, and Bunsen burner)
- Tongs
- Wheat seeds
- Hay (dried grass) from several different places, mixed together
- Dropper pipet (medicine dropper)
- Microscope slides
- Cover slips
- Microscope
- Oven mitts or thermal gloves
- Safety goggles

STEP-BY-STEP

Throughout this investigation, wear your safety goggles whenever you work with hot water.

Day 1

1 Place hay loosely in the large beakers until they are about one-third full. (Do not tightly pack the hay.)

2 Add water until the beakers are about two-thirds full.

3 Heat each beaker on the hot plate or burner until the contents boil. Let them boil for 20 minutes.

4 Carefully use tongs (or oven mitts or thermal gloves) to set the beakers of boiled hay and water aside. Follow your teacher's safety instructions. Cover the beakers loosely, and let them cool.

5 When the beakers are safe to handle, label them with the names of your group members and the date. Label one "Light" and the other "Dark." Then wash your hands with soap and warm water and clean up your work area. (Day 2 of this investigation does not involve any hands-on work.)

Day 3

6 Put water in the 150-mL beaker until it is approximately one-half to two-thirds full.

7 Heat the water. When it begins to boil, add 15–20 wheat seeds.

8 Boil the wheat for two minutes.

9 Using tongs (or wearing oven mitts or thermal gloves), remove the beaker from the heat. Carefully drain the water into the sink, saving the seeds.

10 Add half the seeds and a small handful of fresh, unboiled hay to each large beaker. Replace the covers.

11 Use a dropper pipet to transfer 1 drop of water from the "Dark" beaker to a microscope slide.

12 Add a cover slip, and observe through the microscope, first at low power and then at high power.

13 Use your logbook to record the date and your observations. Include drawings and notes.

14 Rinse off the slide and cover slip.

15 Repeat with a drop taken from the "Light" beaker.

16 Record the date and your observations. Include drawings and notes.

17 Set the "Light" beaker aside in a well-lighted area where it will not be disturbed. Put the "Dark" beaker in a dark cabinet.

18 Wash your hands with soap and warm water before leaving the laboratory.

Days 4–20 *(Continue as long as possible.)*

19 Two or three times a week, use the dropper pipet to take a sample from the surface of the seeds in each beaker. Use a microscope to observe and compare the samples. Every time you make observations, record the date and what you see; also record an estimate of how many of each type of organism you can see at low power and at high power. (Note clearly which observations pertain to each beaker.)

20 Wash your hands with soap and warm water every day before leaving the lab.

Wildfire!

FOREST MANAGER

A forest manager's decisions affect many people: loggers, hunters, fishermen, campers, environmentalists. How a forest is managed also affects its wildlife: If certain kinds of trees are eliminated, the food that some animals need to survive may disappear. The work of a forester involves many biological and ecological issues. Different groups of people often disagree on how a forest should be used, and so foresters must be able to communicate effectively in order to deal with these controversies. It is possible to obtain a two-year associate's degree in forest management, but you stand a much better chance of getting a job in this field if you have a four-year college degree. For more information, provide a self-addressed, stamped return envelope and write:

Agriculture & Natural Resources

Society of American Foresters
Career Information Department
5400 Grosvenor Lane
Bethesda, MD 20814

Related occupations: forest ranger, conservation officer, forest ecologist, tree-nursery operator

TALK IT OVER

Work with the other members of your group to answer the following questions. Make sure all participate in the discussion.

1 Did you see any difference between the two beakers at the beginning of the investigation?

2 Did you see anything in either beaker that might be alive? What evidence is there that what you saw was alive?

3 Did you see any green organisms? If so, did you see more of them in the "Light" beaker or in the "Dark" one? What does the green color suggest to you about how they live?

4 What food and energy resources can you identify in the two beakers? On the basis of your observations, is a food chain present? If so, describe it—which organisms do you think ate which others?

5 How did the kinds and numbers of the different types of organisms change over time? What may have caused these changes?

6 What effect did the light have on the changes that occurred? How may the light have caused these changes?

7 As a forest begins to grow back after a fire, the plant life changes from grass to shrubs to trees. How does this affect the amount of light available near the ground? From what you have seen in your investigation, can changes in the level of light affect the kinds of organisms that grow in an area? Explain.

8 How are the changes you observed similar to what occurs in a forest after a fire?

9 What are some examples of things that people do to slow or prevent natural changes in populations? (Hint: Think about what grows on lawns, on food, or on unpaved roads and paths.)

SPREAD THE WORD

RESULTS

It's time to present the results of your investigation to the rest of the class. Your teacher may have a microscope projector that can help you show how your cultures looked under the microscope. If this piece of equipment is not available, you might set up two or three microscopes to let students see what is growing in your cultures.

When you present your conclusions, describe a few ways that various workers could use what you have discovered.

READ ALL ABOUT IT

The Sun: Source of All Life

SUPPOSE you're in a car, zipping through the countryside with the wind blowing through your hair. You round a curve, and suddenly you're in a forest. . . . What's the first thing you notice? Trees, right? Without trees, there's no forest. The trees and other plants give the forest life. The sunlight that they capture with their leaves provides the energy they use to absorb nutrients from the soil and grow.

Caterpillars, birds, mice, and other animals consume forest vegetation. They are the **primary consumers** in the forest. Owls, foxes, wolves, and other **predators** eat these plant eaters. Predators are the forest's **secondary consumers**.

Every creature in the forest depends on plants for the food energy that makes life on earth possible (see Figure 12, page 60). Because of this important role, plants are called the **primary producers** in the forest community.

It won't surprise you to read that some animals eat plants and that other animals survive by gobbling up smaller creatures. But it may surprise you to learn that only about 10% of the energy available at each level of this food chain reaches the next level: Plant eaters consume only about 10% of the energy captured by plants; predators get only about 10% of the energy consumed by plant eaters. No matter how many levels are in the food chain, the same rule always applies:

10% Rule—About 10% of the energy present on each level of a food chain is consumed by members of the next-higher level.

As you go through a forest, you will see many dead trees and fallen branches on the

Figure 12: Food chain
Note: Plants get energy from the sun. Some animals, such as the chipmunk, consume nuts, seeds, and other plant materials. Animals such as the snake and hawk consume the plant eaters. Dead things and animal wastes are decomposed by worms, beetles, microscopic organisms, and fungi. The nutrients released are absorbed by the soil, providing food for plants to continue the cycle.

ground. What happens to this wood? It does not simply rot away by itself. Fungi and lichens grow on it, and insects or other animals chew it up as they burrow inside.

Other organisms that you can't see, such as bacteria, also help to break down dead material. These organisms, which are called **decomposers**, obtain their nutrients by breaking down dead material, including fallen leaves and branches, animal waste, and dead plants and animals. As they do this, the decomposers release additional nutrients into the soil. Plants use some of the energy they receive from the sun to absorb these nutrients through their roots. As a result, the food chain becomes a cycle: Plants use solar energy to provide power to absorb nutrients . . . some of these nutrients are consumed by animals . . . eventually everything dies and is broken down to basic nutrients, which are reabsorbed by trees and other plants. . . .

This process is extremely important. It allows the forest to survive and grow. Every type of organism in the forest—the primary producer, the animal consumer, and the decomposer—contributes to the cycle as a member of a **biological community**. A biological community is a system that includes all the living things that occupy an area. Nutrients (such as carbon and nitrogen from the air), minerals (such as potassium and phosphorus from the soil), and water are recycled through the community again and again.

GET THIS . . .

According to the 10% Rule, only about 10% of the energy present on each level of a food chain is consumed by members of the next-higher level.

READ ALL ABOUT IT!

Succession: Change in the Forest

WHY do people mow the grass in their yards? Most people would probably say they do it to keep the lawn short and control the weeds. But many people don't realize that mowing the lawn also keeps it from turning into a forest.

When grass is not cut, it grows tall. Eventually, bushes replace the grass, and later trees replace the bushes. This natural process of change is called **succession**. If the soil and climate are suitable and if nothing stops the process, succession can convert grassland to forest.

The process of succession is pictured below (see Figure 13). Grasses and other small plants take root in the sandy soil of the lakeshore. These plants change the environment by shading the ground and providing food for small animals.

Bushes with woody, inedible stems are able to grow well in this new environment, blocking the sunlight needed by the grasses. Soon the bushes replace the grasses almost completely. Later, trees that require shade while they are young sprout under the bushes. When the trees grow tall enough to capture most of the sunlight, the bushes disappear. Over a period of many years, first the grasses, then the bushes, and then the trees spread toward the lake.

Succession also occurs in other settings. For instance, when a support for a new dock is set in the water, various plants, barnacles, or other living things attach themselves to it and begin to grow. This is the beginning of a succession that may lead to a coral reef, with many species of fish, shrimp, and other creatures—or it might just lead to a lot of seaweed, barnacles, and not much else.

What determines the direction that succession will take? To get at the answer to this question, think about these facts: (1) Different kinds of plants grow best in different soils and climates; (2) Adding a source of nutrients affects the growth of microscopic organisms. These two facts have one thing in common: Differences in the environment influence the course of succession. This is true in any kind of

Figure 13: Lakeshore succession

environment, from the bottom of an ocean to the top of a mountain. Succession produces a forest in one place, a grassland in another, and a swamp somewhere else. Why? Because each of these is the kind of community that the environment will support in a particular place. Conifer forests grow better than deciduous forests on acid soil. Tropical rain forests can grow only where the weather is hot and wet all year. The great forests of North America require warm summers and cool winters. In parts of the Midwest, where the weather is too dry to support forests, the natural communities are prairie grasslands.

In any environment the climate, soil type, and slope produce a succession that leads to a community that is more or less stable for hundreds of years. This is called a **climax community**. Exactly what kind of climax community will appear depends on local conditions. Temperature, water supply, sunlight, and the pH and nutrients of the soil all help to determine what kinds of living things can survive in a particular environment. If any of these factors change, the climax community will be disturbed and the process of succession will resume.

What causes succession? Succession occurs when a biological community changes its environment. Eventually the environment may change so much that the original community can no longer survive. For example, some trees require shade when they are young. They can't survive during the early stage in a succession, but later they can grow below shrubs and tall grass. Someday they may grow tall enough to block out the light that other plants need. As time passes, a grassland turns into a forest; grassland animals leave as their food sources disappear; and forest animals replace them.

 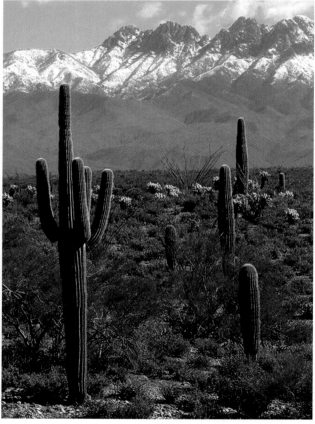

The climax community in a hot, wet climate is a rain forest. Hot, dry climates support only desert vegetation. What climax community would you expect to find in a cool, wet climate?

ON YOUR OWN

Now that you have finished reading "The Sun: Source of All Life" and "Succession: Change in the Forest," use your knowledge of nutrient cycles and succession to give the reasons behind each of the following situations.

1 Farmers and gardeners go to a great deal of trouble to remove weeds (unwanted plants) from their land, but weeds keep coming back.

2 People often pile up dead garden plants, grass clippings, and vegetable peels and let them rot. This forms a material called compost, which they spread on their gardens.

3 Dry grassland (range) is often used for grazing cattle. Range must be burned occasionally to preserve it as a grassland.

4 One way to dispose of sewage sludge is to spread it on farmers' fields. Many farmers would welcome this practice, if they could be sure that the sewage had not been contaminated with toxic materials.

SUCCESSION ON YOUR HEAD?

Have you ever developed an itch, rash, or dandruff after switching to a different brand of shampoo? If this has happened to you, it was probably because the new shampoo changed the environment on the top of your head. A microscopic community of fungi, bacteria, and mites lives on healthy skin. When you changed shampoos, you changed the environment of this tiny community, upsetting the balance among the competing species. The new shampoo may have allowed some of them to increase in numbers—like grass after a forest fire—until they caused an irritation on your scalp. If you started using your old brand of shampoo again, another succession took place, leading back to the earlier community, which did not itch.

ONE FUNGUS AFTER ANOTHER

You've learned how succession takes place among living things. Well, succession occurs on dead material too. Have you ever paid attention to the changes that occur when a fallen log or a piece of fruit decays? A white mold may attack the material at one stage, a green mold at another. Later, bacteria may reduce it to a watery mush. (The photos show three kinds of fungi active during different stages in the decay of a dead tree.) Each community of decomposers changes the material in some way. One decomposer may use up a carbohydrate nutrient; another might produce new waste materials. These changes make the environment less friendly to the community that caused the changes in the first place. But they may make the environment more hospitable to another community. In this way, one decomposer community replaces another one until the material is completely broken down.

Washed-out

EVER WONDER?

After a forest fire, rain that would have landed on leaves splashes directly onto the ground. Will this loosen the soil enough to wash it down gullies and slopes? Does it do any harm when some soil does wash away? Does the shape of the land—whether it is flat or hilly—affect how much soil washes away?

Water reshapes the landscape. In this investigation you will see if the amount of soil that washes away is the same on different slopes of land. You will also learn how vegetation affects the amount of soil that is washed away.

MATERIALS LIST

- Section of U-shaped roofing gutter (1 or 2 m long)
- Rubber tubing to attach to spigot
- Wooden blocks (various sizes)
- Plastic funnel that will fit inside roofing gutter
- Soil
- Sand
- Clay
- 3 small potted plants
- Protractor

STEP-BY-STEP

In this investigation you will examine several variables that affect how soil is washed away. These variables include slope, soil material, and plant cover.

1 Set up a stream table as shown in Figure 14.

2 Get a steady stream of water moving down the channel into the sink. *Caution: Don't run the water too fast—it might spill onto the floor and cause someone to slip.*

3 Have one group member use the protractor to measure and record the slope of the stream channel. (**Math tip:** If you need help understanding how a protractor is used to measure angles, ask your teacher. Knowing how to use a protractor is important in mathematics.)

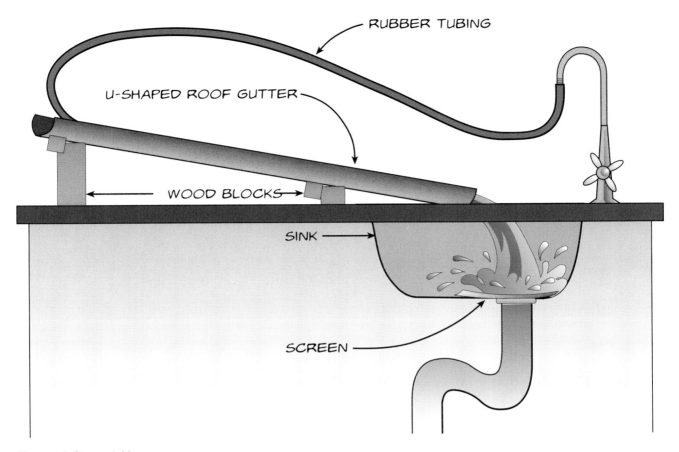

Figure 14: Stream table

4 Turn off the stream of water.

5 You will now use different materials to make some "mountains." Work over a wastebasket or sink, and follow your teacher's directions. Begin by filling a funnel with soil. Pack in the soil tightly. You may need to add a small amount of water to help it stick together.

6 Put the funnel upside down in the channel, and then gently lift it up, leaving a soil "mountain." You may need to tap the funnel gently to release the soil before lifting the funnel.

7 Turn on the water. Record the time.

8 Watch as the water washes away some of the soil. As your mountain erodes, record the changes that you see. Also record the time each change occurs. Continue timing until half (or all) of the mountain collapses or washes away.

9 Turn off the water.

10 Perform Steps 5–9 two more times.

11 Calculate the average time it took for half (or all) of the mountain to collapse or wash away. Record the average. (**Math tip:** To find the average, add up the times and divide by three.)

Wildfire!

12 Gently loosen one plant and its attached soil, and remove it all from the pot.

13 Place the plant and its soil in the channel.

14 Turn on the water. Record the time.

15 Observe as the water washes away some of the soil. As the soil erodes, record the changes that you see. Also record the time each change occurs. Continue timing until half (or all) of the soil washes away.

16 Turn off the water

17 Use each of the other plants, and perform Steps 12–16 two more times.

18 Calculate the average time it took for half (or all) of the soil to wash away. Record the average.

19 Change the block supporting the stream channel to create a new slope.

20 Have one member of your group use the protractor to measure and record the new slope.

21 Repeat Steps 5–11, using the new slope.

22 If time permits, repeat Steps 5–11, using sand.

23 If time permits, repeat Steps 5–11, using clay.

24 Wash your hands, and follow your teacher's cleanup directions.

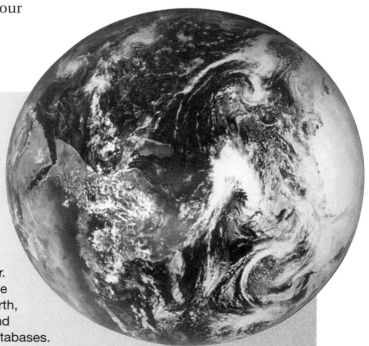

SKY-HIGH TECH

If you're thinking about a career in forest or land management, you ought to be thinking about satellites and computers too.

Knowing how to use satellite-assisted computers is becoming a necessity for anyone interested in becoming a park ranger, fish and wildlife manager, or forester. Workers entering these fields should be able to use satellites to pinpoint locations on earth, and to access the vast amounts of land- and weather-related information in computer databases.

Where can you get this kind of training? One place is Hocking College in Nelsonville, Ohio, which offers a two-year program leading to an associate's degree in Global Positioning Systems and Geographic Information Systems. (This training can also be used in careers involving city planning; police, fire, and medical work; and even battlefield tactics.)

Science L i n k s

TALK IT OVER

Work with the other members of your group to answer the following questions.

1 How would you measure the amount of soil that washed from one end of the stream channel to the other? If possible, repeat one of the experiments, and put your ideas to work in measuring the amount of soil that moves.

2 What effect does vegetation have on the amount of soil that is eroded?

3 What effect does the slope of the land have on the amount of soil that is eroded?

4 What effect does the type of "mountain" material have on the rate that soil washes away?

5 If you were the manager of a forest preserve, what actions would you take after a forest fire to prevent rainwater from washing the soil away?

CAREER LINKS

SOIL-CONSERVATION AGENT

What kinds of soil are most likely to be washed away? This is a question for a soil-conservation agent. This person may oversee the classification of the different types of soil in a given area to determine the risk of erosion and to suggest how different pieces of land should be used. The work often involves educating the public at meetings and "field days" on the farm or in the woods. This career requires a degree from a college of agriculture. Conservation agents must know biology and math, and they need good interpersonal and communication skills. For more information, write:

Agriculture & Natural Resources

U.S. Forest Service

Soil and Water Conservation Society
7515 N.E. Ankeny Road
Ankeny, IA 50021
http://www.netins.net/showcase/swcs

Related occupations: farmer, landscape architect, civil engineer, golf-course designer

SPREAD THE WORD

Present the results of your investigation to the class. It would be helpful to other students if you demonstrated how the stream channel works. Also tell the class about some occupations in which workers must protect soil.

Explain how foresters who are planning the restoration of a burned forest could take advantage of your conclusions. Discuss some other occupations in which workers must prevent soil losses.

Wildfire!

It's a Wash

AFTER a fire burns through a forest, succession might return to an early stage, as grasses and other small, fast-growing plants begin to cover the ground. During this stage, the whole area may be at risk.

The process by which water, wind, or ice moves soil (and other material that collects on the earth's surface) is called **erosion**. Erosion moves soil and reshapes the landscape. Land can be eroded whether it is flat or hilly. The slant or incline of the land's surface is called its **slope**.

Rocks are much harder than water, but water can wear away the hardest rocks—it just takes time. It has taken the Colorado River millions of years to carve the Grand Canyon. That's erosion on a grand scale.

Erosion plays an important role in the process of succession. Without the cover of leaves to protect the soil, raindrops splash directly onto the ground. This loosens the soil particles, making it easier for rain or melting snow to wash away the rich surface soil and its supply of plant nutrients. If this soil is lost, plant growth will be poor, and the forest may take years longer to recover. That's why it is sometimes necessary to replant a forest soon after a fire.

Steeper slopes erode quickly, because the runoff water gains speed and power as it flows downhill. In other words, runoff washes away more soil on slopes than on flatter ground.

Erosion is a major force in shaping the land. The Grand Canyon is an extreme example of erosion: Over millions of years, the water of the Colorado River has worn away the rock, carving a massive canyon out of the land.

ON YOUR OWN

Answer the following questions based on "It's a Wash."

1 Many farmers practice minimum-tillage agriculture, which means they hardly ever plow the soil. Instead, after they harvest one crop, they simply drop seeds and fertilizer for the next crop into a narrow slit in the ground. A layer of dead stems and leaves from the

previous crop is left on the ground instead of being plowed into the soil. How do you think the rate of erosion would change in a field if a farmer switched from regular plowing to minimum tillage?

2 Where do you think a house would be least likely to have the soil washed out from under its foundation: on a hilltop, on the side of a hill, or on flat ground? Explain your reasons.

3 What are some ways that you could protect a house on a hillside from damage by soil erosion?

SECTION WRAP-UP

The World Keeps Changing

ALMOST all life on earth is powered by the sun. Energy from the sun is captured by plant leaves and is converted to chemical energy in the form of carbohydrates and other materials that make up plant tissue. After wood and other plant material dies, approximately 90% of it is broken down by decomposers, such as insects, earthworms, fungi, and bacteria. The remaining 10% is consumed by animals. In turn, these animals are consumed by other animals. This is a food chain, and such a chain can have many links or levels.

RECYCLING NUTRIENTS

According to the 10% Rule, each level of the food chain receives about 10% of the energy available from the level below. Plants, animals, fungi, and microscopic organisms all die and are broken down by the decomposers to soil nutrients, which are absorbed by the roots of plants. Nutrients cycle from plants to animals and decomposers in a biological community, which consists of all the living things in an area.

Every biological community changes the environment in some way—for instance, by consuming soil minerals, adding organic matter to the soil, or blocking sunlight. As the environment changes, other organisms begin to enter and dominate the community. Eventually this can produce a completely different community. For example, a meadow may become a forest. This process of change is called succession. Succession occurs in

Primary consumers, including this rabbit, receive 10% of the energy available from plants. Secondary consumers, including the coyote, get 10% of the energy available from plant eaters. Animal wastes and the remains of dead plants and animals are broken down by decomposers, returning nutrients to the soil.

every type of biological community, including forests, oceans, vacant lots, and even the surface of plants, animals, and humans. If an area is not disturbed by people, floods, fires, or weather, succession will eventually lead to a more or less stable climax community. People often try to stop this process because they want one species to dominate, as in a lawn with only one species of grass or in a farm field with a single crop.

Every species has an ideal pH range in which it is most successful.

The kinds of communities that succession produces depend greatly on the physical environment: the climate, the soil type, and the chemical makeup of the soil and water. Soil and water pH are important factors in the environment. Acids, which produce hydrogen ions (H^+), reduce the pH, and bases, which produce hydroxyl ions (OH^-), raise the pH.

Every species has an ideal pH range in which it is most successful. Most species live in moderately acidic environments, with soil and water pH in the range of 5.5–6.8. Too much acid can reduce the pH of soil and water until forest and pond life disappear. Acid rain can do this.

Most of the mineral nutrients that plants extract from soil are bases. When a forest burns, these bases remain in the ashes and are washed back into the soil by rain. After a fire, rain may also wash away soil because plants on the ground have burned and can no longer protect the soil. This erosion reduces the nutrient resources that are available to the plants, which support the entire biological community. It can also have other effects. For instance, the washed-away soil may clog creeks and rivers.

Burned trees . . . blankets of ashes. . . . After a forest fire, the landscape looks dead, but a new forest may rise from the ashes of the old.

ON YOUR OWN

Answer the following questions based on "The World Keeps Changing."

1 Suppose an intense fire burns a forest-covered hillside but then heavy rains, which last several days, put out the fire. How do you think the forest succession would be affected by the fire and rain?

2 Natural communities, such as forests, keep themselves going without help. But many farmers add manure or chemical fertilizers to their fields nearly every year. Why?

3 Do you think an acid paint might help protect wooden buildings from mildew, termites, and other organisms that attack wood? Give your reasons.

4 Would you expect the pH of a forest soil to be higher before a fire or afterward? Explain why you think so.

Wildfire!—A Study of Heat and Oxidation

FORESTS grow where the soil and the climate allow them to grow. If there is enough rainfall and if temperatures do not get extremely cold, trees can compete well against grasses and other plants. What causes differences in climate from place to place? In this module you have learned about two factors that are important in shaping climate: (1) the specific heat of water, and (2) the amount of heat energy that is needed to make water evaporate.

Because water has such a high specific heat, any moisture in trees and soil will increase the amount of heat that they must gain or lose before they can change temperature. This tends to reduce extremes of heat and cold; in other words, it helps create a more stable climate in which temperatures do not change drastically. In contrast, an extremely dry area, such as a treeless desert, tends to have very hot days and very cold nights.

Climate determines which kinds of vegetation grow in a particular region. In an area that receives only a small amount of moisture, the process of succession may lead to a grassland. But wet areas are likely to produce forests. The Pacific Northwest, for example, receives cool, moist air, thanks to breezes carrying water that evaporated from the ocean. This produces the mild temperatures of Oregon and Washington. The coastal climate has helped shape succession to produce a temperate rain forest climax community.

In an area that receives only a small amount of moisture, the process of succession may lead to a grassland.

Specific heat, along with convection, also plays an important role in coastal weather patterns. The morning sun heats the land more than the water (because the land has a lower specific heat than the ocean). During the day, warm, moist air rises from the land, causing wind to blow onshore from the ocean. At night the land cools down more quickly than the ocean, reversing the pattern: Cool air sinks toward the ground and blows out to sea.

TAKING THE HEAT
Once you know that it takes a large amount of heat energy to make water evaporate, you can understand why the moisture in wood helps to prevent forest fires. Trees must get hotter than the boiling point of the water inside them before they will burn well. Hot, dry weather makes it more likely that a fire will break out, because such conditions cause the moisture in wood (living or dead)

The danger of forest fire increases in hot, dry weather. Such conditions cause the water inside wood to evaporate, making it easier for wood to burn.

Science L i n k s

to evaporate. As wood dries, its heat capacity falls—less heat is needed to raise its temperature. The wood can then easily heat up. This adds fuel and heat to the oxygen in the air, completing the fire triangle. Now heat energy begins to promote a chemical reaction between the wood and the oxygen. This oxidation, which is called fire, releases energy in the form of heat and light.

As more heat is produced, the fire burns faster. Heat speeds up most chemical reactions, including oxidation. In a forest fire, oxygen and fuel come in contact with each other at the surfaces of branches, leaves, and other vegetation. Small twigs and leaves burn quickly, because they have more surface area per gram of fuel. Large tree limbs and trunks burn more slowly—they have less surface area per gram of fuel exposed to heat and oxygen.

UP IN FLAMES

Through heat convection, burning gases and debris can rapidly carry surface fires up to the tops of trees. If this process ignites the flammable oils and resins in conifer needles, a dangerous crown fire can result. Heat conduction along branches can also spread the flames, and radiation of heat energy may be intense enough to ignite more trees.

Another feature that fire shares with most other chemical reactions is that the rate at which it occurs depends on its supply of reactants. If a forest hasn't burned in many years, the ground may be cluttered with dead trees and branches. This added fuel supply increases the rate at which the wood burns, as well as the intensity of the heat that the fire produces.

A forest fire usually does not destroy all the trees in the forest. After a blaze, patches of

DON'T START WHAT YOU CAN'T STOP

You can have a great time around a campfire in the woods—but be careful! Here are some tips for preventing forest fires:

- Check on fire conditions before you leave for the forest.

- Don't park on dry grass or brush, even for a minute! Your vehicle's exhaust system can reach a temperature of more than 538°C, but it takes only 260°C to start a wildfire during fire season.

- Before lighting your campfire, clear all vegetation, fallen leaves and branches, and other debris within a radius of three meters (about 10 feet).

- Keep a shovel or bucket handy in case the fire starts to get out of control.

- When it's time to put out the fire, turn it into a mud puddle. Stir water and dirt into the hot coals by using a shovel or stick. Make sure the fire is dead before you leave—the ashes should be cold enough to touch with your bare hands.

- Be extra careful if people are smoking. Be sure they extinguish their cigarettes only in cleared areas where there's no vegetation or debris.

- Never use fireworks in the forest.

undamaged or partially burned trees may still be standing next to areas that sustained heavy damage. An occasional fire is actually beneficial to a forest community. This is true because trees, as they grow, remove bases and other nutrients from the ground, leaving many forest soils acidic and poor in nutrients. Because of a fire, much of the nutrient supply returns to the soil in the form of ashes. Furthermore, sunlight can now enter burned areas that used

Wildfire!

to be shaded by trees. This allows new and different plants to grow.

Some seeds can sprout only after they've been exposed to the heat of a forest fire. The new growth provides food for forest animals. Fungi, insects, and other decomposers begin to break down dead trees and other organic material that the fire killed. The process of decomposition releases nutrients to the soil, where plant roots absorb them.

Succession begins again in the burned areas, as new plants benefit from the bases and nutrients in the ashes and debris left from the fire.

In many cases succession produces a restored forest similar to the one that burned. However, if plants do not cover the ground soon after a fire, the area may be seriously damaged by rain or by runoff water from rain or melting snow.

FIGHT FIRE WITH . . .

Sometimes people fight fire with fire, but most of the time, for small fires, they need fire extinguishers. The kind of extinguisher you need depends on the material that is burning.

There are four classes of fires:

- **Class A**—paper, wood, clothing, rubber, and other solid items
- **Class B**—flammable liquids and gases, such as cooking grease and gasoline
- **Class C**—electrical switches, motors, and other equipment
- **Class D**—combustible metals, such as magnesium

There are many types of extinguishers, but the three main ones are:

- **Water extinguishers**—Class A fires (These contain only water and should never be used to fight electrical fires.)

- **Dry-chemical extinguishers**— Class B and C fires (If the extinguisher contains a multi-purpose chemical, it can also be used on Class A fires. Read the label.)

- **Liquefied-gas extinguishers**— Class B fires

To fight a Class D fire, you need a special extinguisher designed for the particular kind of metal that is burning.

Plant leaves form a protective canopy that protects the soil from the direct impact of raindrops. Roots also help hold soil particles together. Rainfall can loosen soil particles, and these particles can then wash away when water runs over the surface. Such runoff cuts small rills in the ground, and these may widen to form large gullies. Erosion such as this can make enormous changes in the landscape. It can cut deep gullies in slopes, and it can wash away valuable plant nutrients that support life in the forest.

The loss of these nutrients makes the soil less fertile. This slows down the process of

Forest fires, soil erosion, weather changes . . . all involve heat and oxidation. They're all linked!

succession and changes its direction. If severe erosion takes place after a fire, the forest may never recover. Whether succession leads to another forest, a grassland, or a meadow, the major changes that take place in a biological community because of a fire may also change the area's climate. For example, trees in a forest shade the soil, helping to conserve groundwater by reducing evaporation, but if a grassland replaces the forest, the area may become drier.

Forest fires, soil erosion, weather changes . . . in one way or another, they all involve heat and oxidation. They're all linked!

ON YOUR OWN

Answer the following questions based on the Module Wrap-up.

1 Many forest soils are covered with a layer of flammable material, such as damp, decaying wood and leaves. Only the most intense forest fires destroy much of this material or kill many of the fungi, plants, and animals found in it. How would you explain the survival of this decomposer community? Be sure to mention all the factors you think are important.

2 After cutting and burning forestland to make a new field, farmers often find that their crops grow well for a few years but then produce less and less. To continue harvesting large crops, farmers must add fertilizer (plant nutrients) and ground limestone (a base) to the soil. Why do the crops grow well for the first few years? Why do the fields need fertilizer a few years after the forest is cleared? Would large chunks of limestone be just as useful as ground limestone? Explain your ideas.

3 Suppose a forest fire begins with a certain amount of wood, either as a few big trunks and logs or as many small twigs and branches. Which would produce more heat per minute? Which would spread faster? Explain your answers. Also explain how heat transfer would differ in the two cases.

4 The Sierra Nevada is a tall mountain range that runs north and south near the border of California and Nevada. The western slope of these mountains is covered with forests and thick stands of grass. East of the Sierras, desert extends for hundreds of miles. What explanation can you give for the difference between the California forests and the Nevada desert?

Wildfire!

How to Use Your Logbook

ALL through *Science Links* you will use a logbook to keep records of your work. A logbook is an important tool in scientific investigation. It provides a place to take notes, collect data, enter observations and conclusions, and jot down questions and ideas. Most scientists keep a log like this one.

In science it is essential to keep accurate records. The information that you collect is valuable—you must work to get it! So write down your ideas before you forget them.

Your logbook will also help you share your ideas with other students. In most of your investigations, you will work as a member of a group. In any situation where people must work together, whether it's flying a jetliner or leading cheers at a basketball game, teamwork is critical. One of the most important aspects of teamwork is communication. No team can succeed unless its members communicate effectively with one another.

GOOD WRITING IS CLEAR AND SIMPLE

Effective communication means writing and speaking in ways that other people will understand. Your logbook can help you develop a good writing style. Whenever you make an entry, try to express your thoughts as clearly and simply as possible. When you finish writing, step back and look at the words as though you are reading them for the first time. If someone else had made this entry, would you be able to understand it? Is the writing clear? Does it cover all the points it was supposed to? You know what you meant to say, but did you succeed in saying it? If you have any doubts, go back to work on the entry.

Writing makes you more aware of your thinking process. This is useful in science because sometimes you don't even realize that you do not understand a concept until you try to express it. Communicating scientific ideas through writing and discussion helps you understand what you are doing. And in *Science Links* the emphasis is on doing science.

Your logbook gives you an opportunity to show your teacher what you have learned. It will reveal how you and the other members of your group are collaborating. The notes you take during presentations by other groups will show if you are receiving useful information from them.

ORGANIZING YOUR LOGBOOK

Your logbook should be organized chronologically. Every time you make a new entry, put the date in the upper left-hand corner of the page. Next, in the upper right-hand corner, write a few words that tell what the entry is about. Then write the entry itself. (A sample entry appears on the next page.)

Various types of entries are possible. Here are some of them:

- notes based on what occurs during procedures (**Step-by-Step**)

- summaries of group or class discussions (**Talk It Over**)

- outlines for presentations by your group (**Spread the Word**)

- notes and questions about presentations by other groups

- data collected through research

- ideas for projects or reports

- personal views concerning *Science Links* activities

Use your logbook regularly. It will help you keep track of and understand the science you are doing in *Science Links*.

September 30, 1998

Step-by-Step

Step 4	baking soda & paper	5.46 g
	paper	−3.46
	baking soda	2.00 g

Step 9	beaker & contents	123.76 g
Step 12	beaker & contents after reaction	−122.31
	weight lost	1.45 g

After Kim poured the vinegar in the beaker, it foamed up. Giselle said it smelled sour.

Step 14	baking soda & paper	4.83 g
	paper	−2.83
	baking soda	2.00 g

Step 21	bottle & contents	90.50 g
Step 23	beaker & contents after reaction	−90.30
	weight lost	0.20 g

After I poured the vinegar out, it foamed up.

Talk It Over

#1–4. Everybody agreed that the beaker lost more weight than the bottle. Kim said this was because something turned into a gas and it went out of the beaker but couldn't get out of the bottle.

Module Glossary

acid—a substance that increases the concentration of hydrogen ions (53)

base—a substance that increases the concentration of hydroxyl ions or that reduces the concentration of hydrogen ions (53)

biological community—a system composed of all the living things in an area, including primary producers, primary and secondary consumers, and decomposers (61)

catalyst—a substance that increases the rate of a reaction but is not changed by that reaction (10)

climax community—a biological community that is more or less stable over many hundreds of years, unless disturbed by changes in climate or other outside forces (62)

condensation—a phase change from gas to liquid (42)

conduction—the transfer of heat energy by contact (36)

convection—the tendency of hot fluids to rise and of cooler fluids to sink (36)

control—in an experiment, the sample that the experimenter does not change in any way and that serves as the standard with which the experimental samples are compared (8)

decomposer—a species that obtains nutrients and energy from dead material (60)

enzyme—a complex protein, produced by living cells, that catalyzes biochemical reactions at body temperatures (10)

erosion—the process by which water, wind, or ice moves soil and other material on the earth's surface (68)

evaporation—a phase change from solid or liquid to gas; boiling is a rapid type of evaporation (42)

freezing—a phase change from liquid to solid (43)

heat—the energy associated with the moving particles (atoms or molecules) in matter when that energy is transferred from one particle to another (35)

heat capacity—the amount of heat that an object absorbs or releases when its temperature changes by 1°C (Heat Capacity = Specific Heat x Mass) (23)

ideal environment—the right combination of climate, soil, nutrients, light, and other factors for a particular species (5)

Law of Conservation of Matter—matter cannot be created or destroyed in a chemical reaction (19)

melting—a phase change from solid to liquid (42)

neutral—neither acidic nor basic; a substance, such as pure water, with a pH of 7 (53)

oxidation—a chemical change in which a substance combines with oxygen (9)

phase change—the process that occurs when matter changes from one form to another, such as from solid to liquid (42)

pioneer species—any of the first species to enter an area where there is no living biological community, such as after a fire or on newly exposed soil; most pioneer species are primary producers or decomposers (53)

predator—a species that obtains energy and nutrients by killing and consuming other organisms; most predators are animals (59)

primary producer—a species that obtains its energy from nonbiological sources, such as sunlight; most primary producers are plants (59)

primary consumer—a species that obtains energy and nutrients from primary producers (59)

product—any substance that is produced during a chemical change (10)

radiation—production of energy rays that spread out and travel without having to be carried by any substance (37)

rate of chemical reaction—the amount of a reactant that changes to products per unit of time (10)

reactant—any substance that undergoes a chemical change (9)

secondary consumer—a species that obtains energy and nutrients from primary consumers (59)

slope—the slant, grade, or incline of the land's surface (68)

specific heat—the amount of heat that must be added to one gram of a substance to increase its temperature by 1°C (22)

succession—the natural process of change in which one biological community replaces another (61)

temperature—a measurement of the average energy of the moving atoms and molecules that are present in all matter (35)

10% Rule—the typical pattern that exists in many biological communities whereby approximately 10% of the weight of primary producers is consumed by primary consumers, 10% of the weight of primary consumers is consumed by secondary consumers, and so on; the other 90% includes living tissue, animal waste, and dead material that is broken down by decomposers (59)

For Further Study . . .

BOOKS AND ARTICLES

Cottrell, W.H. Jr. 1989. *The Book of Fire.* Missoula, MT: Mountain Press.

Gerber, B.L., and E.A. Marek. 1996. Energy efficient architecture. *The Science Teacher* 63: 25–27. (This article deals with heat transfer.)

Green, T. 1996. Watershed science: analyzing chemical changes in water as it interacts with soil. *The Science Teacher* 63: 34–36.

HAZWRAP (Hazardous Waste Remedial Actions Program). *Try Out Soda Bottle Hydrology.* Washington, DC: U.S. Department of Energy, Office of Environmental Restoration.

Lauber, P. 1991. *Summer of Fire: Yellowstone 1988.* New York: Orchard Books.

MacGregor, B. 1994. *Wildfire Classroom Activities: Fire Education Activities for Grades 6–9.* Washington State Department of Natural Resources.

Pernin, P. 1971. *The Great Peshtigo Fire: An Eyewitness Account.* Madison, WI: State Historical Society of Wisconsin. (This work was originally published in 1874 in Montreal as *The Finger of God Is There!, or Thrilling Episode of a Strange Event Related by an Eye-Witness, Rev. P. Pernin, United States Missionary.* It is also available on tape from the State Historical Society of Wisconsin.)

Pringle, L. 1995. *Fire in the Forest: A Cycle of Growth and Renewal.* New York: Simon & Schuster.

Stevens, W.K. 1995. *Miracle under the Oaks.* New York: Simon & Schuster.

Williams, J. 1992. *The Weather Book: An Easy-to-Understand Guide to the USA's Weather.* Arlington, VA: National Science Teachers Association.

Zucca, C., W. Harris, and B. Anderson. 1995. Forest fire ecology. *The Science Teacher* 62: 23–25.

INTERNET

Agency for Instructional Technology (AIT):

• World Wide Web—http://www.ait.net

• *Technos,* a journal for education and technology—technos@ait.net

South-Western Science:

• World Wide Web— http://science.swep.com

• Science Discussion List—To join, send an e-mail message to majordomo@list.thomson.com and in the body of the message include the words *subscribe swep–science.*

VIDEO

BioQuest (CD-ROM). This collection of software simulations for biology, includes two items that are relevant to Module 2: "Environmental Decision Making" and "Rate It!" (enzyme kinetics). It is available from Academic Software Development Group, BioQuest Library, Computer Science Center, Building 224, University of Maryland, College Park, MD 20742.

The Dynamic Forest (videotape). Produced by the Temperate Forest Foundation, this tape shows how forests are shaped, how they function, and how they can be managed for current and future generations. Write the foundation at 14780 S.W. Osprey Drive, Suite 355, Beaverton, OR 97007.

Everything Weather (CD-ROM). This CD-ROM contains a climatological database for more than 700 cities. It includes a weather glossary, in-depth storm analysis, photos and videos of all major weather phenomena, and several interactive activities. Users may access the latest weather forecasts for 200 cities. It is available from the Weather Channel.

Tropical Regions and Rainforests (videotape). This 15-minute program from *Life on Our Planet* in the Science Source series was produced by AIT. Topics include major climatic regions, latitude, and temperature. It is available from AIT. Call 1-800-457-4509.

U.S.D.A. Forest Service Library. Schools may borrow videos from this library by contacting the distributor, Audience Planners, 5341 Derry Avenue, Suite Q, Agoura Hills, CA 91301. The web site is http://www.fs.fed.us; or phone: (800) 683-8366.

Wilderness (videotape). This 20-minute program from AIT's *Interactions in Science and Society* deals with the nature and preservation of wilderness. It is available from AIT. Call 1-800-457-4509.

Learning Tools

EnviroScape II (model). A three-dimensional interactive model of a watershed, this device can be used to demonstrate water pollution and its prevention. It measures 25"x30"x5" and includes a kit with all materials needed to demonstrate the movement of water through a watershed and the pollution that runoff may cause. For more information, contact EnviroScape c/o JT&A, Inc., Washington, DC.

Project Learning Tree: Environmental Education for the '90s (school project). Cosponsored by the American Forest Foundation and the Western Regional Environmental Education Council, this project is designed for students in preschool through high school. It uses the forest as a window onto the natural world, helping students gain awareness and knowledge of the world and their place in it.

The Science of Flames (poster). This full-color poster illustrates the composition of flames, the process of combustion, and radiation of energy. On the back are lesson plans, activities, and experiments. It is available from the National Science Teachers Association, Arlington, VA.

Agencies and Organizations

American Gas Association. Posters and other materials on combustion are available from this organization, located at 1515 Wilson Boulevard, Arlington, VA 22209.

Bureau of Land Management. This agency, a branch of the U.S. Department of the Interior, can provide materials, including a book about fire ecology. Contact this office of the bureau: Environmental Education and Volunteers Team; 1849 C Street, N.W. (LS-1275), Washington, DC 20240.

Department of Natural Resources. Contact your state agency for information and materials on fire and other subjects involving forests. Look under "Government Offices, State" in the yellow pages.

U.S.D.A. Forest Service. Smokey the Bear, played by a forest ranger, likes to visit classrooms and give demonstrations to students. Brochures and other materials are also available. Contact the Forest Service. For the phone number, look under "Government Offices, U.S." in the yellow pages.

1,500 Die in a 'Sea of Flame'

THE deadliest forest fire in American history occurred near Green Bay, Wisconsin, in 1871. More than 1,500 persons died in the blaze; 2,400 square miles of land burned; and several villages were completely destroyed.

An eyewitness account of this catastrophe, which is known as the Great Peshtigo Fire, was written by Father Peter Pernin, a missionary priest who was serving the towns of Green Bay and Peshtigo and who barely survived the fire. The following four paragraphs, which describe the fire in vivid detail, are adapted from his journal, which he later published.

Immense numbers of fish died, and the following morning the river was covered with them. It would be impossible to decide what was the cause of their death. It may have been owing to the intensity of the heat, or the lack of air necessary to maintain life, the air having been violently sucked in by the movement upward to that fierce center of flames, or they may have been killed by some poisonous gas. . . .

While standing in the river [during the fire], I had noticed, on casting my eye upwards, a sea of flame, whose waves were in violent motion, rolling over one another, and all at a great height in the sky, and

therefore far from any material that might burn.

Generally speaking, those people who happened to be in low-lying lands, especially close to dug-up places or freshly ploughed earth with which they could cover themselves, as the Indians do, succeeded in saving their lives. Most frequently, the path of fire passed at a certain height from the earth, touching only the highest places. Thus, no one could meet it standing up without almost instant death. . . .

When the fire came upon us, many, surprised and terrified, ran out to see what was the matter. A number of these persons say that they witnessed something marvelous. They saw a large black object, resembling a balloon, which revolved in the air at great speed, advancing above the trees. Barely had it touched a house when the "balloon" burst with a loud noise, like a bomb, and at the same time, streams of fire poured out in all directions. With the speed of thought, the house was completely wrapped in flame, inside and out. . . .

—Adapted from *The Great Peshtigo Fire: An Eyewitness Account* by Peter Pernin, originally published in 1874 in Montreal as *The Finger of God Is There!, or Thrilling Episode of a Strange Event Related by an Eye-Witness, Rev. P. Pernin, United States Missionary*. For more information see Appendix C, page 80.

> **A number of these persons say that they witnessed something marvelous. They saw a large black object, resembling a balloon, which revolved in the air at great speed. . . . the "balloon" burst with a loud noise, like a bomb . . . streams of fire poured out in all directions.**

WISCONSIN

Peshtigo

Green Bay

Wildfire!

K

Kiev, 45

killing frost, 41

kindling point, 40

L

Law of Conservation of Matter,
     19, 24–25

logbook, vi, 76–77

London, 45

Los Angeles, 44

M

Massachusetts, 34, 44

Mediterranean Sea, 5

melting, 28, 41–42, 47

Mexico, 5

Minnesota, 4

Muir, John, 56

N

neutral, 52–54

Nevada, 75

New Dehli, 45

New Hampshire, 4, 34

New York, 4, 54

nitrogen, 61

North Dakota, 4

North Sea, 45

nutrient cycle, 60–61, 63, 69

O

Ohio, 66

Oregon, 72

oxidation:
     defined, 9, 24
     mentioned, 25–26, 73, 75
     rates of, 9–10, 24
     rust, 9–10, 15, 24

oxyacetylene torch, 10

oxygen:
     and fire, 9–10, 14, 24–25,
          72–73
     mentioned, 6–7, 11, 53

P

Pacific Northwest, 72

Pennsylvania, 4

Pernin, Peter, 82

Peshtigo, Wisconsin, 82

petroleum, 40

pH, 50–54, 62, 70–71

phase change:
     definition of, 42
     and fire, 46, 47
     mentioned, 27, 38, 40, 43
     and weather, 44

phases of matter, 42, 46

phosphorus, 61

pioneer species, 53

potassium, 61

predators, 59

primary consumers, 59

primary producers, 59, 61

producers. *See* primary
     producers

products, 10–11, 14, 19, 25

R

radiation:
     definition of, 36–37, 46
     heat, 37
     light, 36
     mentioned, 32, 35, 45, 73
     nuclear, 37
     solar, 44
     and weather, 44, 47

rain. *See* rainfall

rainfall:
     and erosion, 68, 70, 74
     map, 3
     mentioned, 52, 64
     patterns of, 2
     and phase change, 47
     and soil nutrients, 53
     and succession, 71–72
     and sun, 45
     and water, 45–46
     and wind, 4

rate of chemical reaction. *See*
     chemical reaction, rate of

reactants:
     concentration of, 10, 14, 24,
          73
     defined, 9–10
     mentioned, 11, 25
     surface area of, 15, 24

S

safety symbols:
     described, vii

San Francisco, 44

satellites and satellite-assisted
     computers, 66

secondary consumers, 59

Siberia, 18

Sierra Nevada, 75

slope:
     and erosion, 64, 67–68
     mentioned, 47, 66
     and succession, 62

··

ILLUSTRATIONS AND PHOTOS

··

Illustration Credits— Mike Cagle, 3, 7, 13, 14, 30, 31, 36, 37, 42, 61, 65; Brenda Grannan, icons; Vance Lawry, 60

Photo Credits—James A. Christiansen, Ph.D., National College of Chiropractic, Lombard, IL, 37; Corel Corporation, 22, 26, 36, 41, 44, 52, 59, 62 (desert), 63, 66, 68 (Grand Canyon), 69, 74; David Gudaitis, 62 (rain forest); Debbie Hanna, 10, 68 (tractor); Brian Lynch, Irish Tourist Board, 4; Jim Peaco, Yellowstone National Park, 1, 38, 46, 48, 72; Softkey, 43